T0168266

IN SEARCH OF THE PAPER TIGER

IN SEARCH OF THE PAPER TIGER:

A Sociological Perspective of Myth, Formula and the Mystery Genre in the Entertainment Print Mass Medium

Gary C. Hoppenstand

Bowling Green State University Popular Press
Bowling Green, Ohio 43403

Acknowledgments

The author would like to gratefully acknowledge Ray and Pat Browne for their support and guidance of this project, and Garyn G. Roberts for his expert advice.

Copyright © 1987 by Bowling Green State University Popular Press

Library of Congress Catalogue Card No.: 86-72355

ISBN: 0-87972-355-6 Clothbound
      0-87972-356-4 Paperback

CONTENTS

PREFACE

SCHOLARSHIP IS LIKE A STEP-LADDER that everyone must climb in order to see over his or her predecessors. Major works are like the main rungs in the step-ladder and must be experienced and crossed. But though each one must be stood on, hopefully the standing on is for a brief span while the scholar does his or her own independent thinking and then progresses onto the next rung, and so on *ad infinitum*.

In American scholarship in popular culture there are certain ladder-rungs which spring to mind immediately: Henry Nash Smith's *Virgin Land*, Richard Slotkin's *Regeneration Through Violence*, Russel B. Nye's *The Unembarrassed Muse*, Daniel Boorstin's *The Image: A Guide to Pseudo-Events in America*, John Cawelti's *Six-Gun Mystique* (and his subsequent *Adventure, Mystery and Romance*) and Alan Gowans' *Learning to See*. Doubtless there are others that individuals will name as the useful books in their growing-up. All these works had eye-opening and mind-expanding properties. They were truly educational in opening not only the road to the use of new materials but also in the real concepts of ways that materials could fruitfully be used.

But these works, helpful as they had been, were merely stepping stones, rungs on the ladder, to the development of the mind that truly sought to know about the phenomenon of human nature and human society. They were to be used, treasured—and placed on the shelf for occasional reference, not tamped in the head for mental baggage that could encumber as much as assist. For, properly used, books are to be stood *on* not stood *under*. They are to make mankind stand taller, not slump over under their weight. Books are chain-cutters that allow mankind to rise up, not great weights that hold mankind down, manacled to the ideas and methods of yesterday and yesteryear, proud to be stuffed with the ideas of others but afraid to stand alone with their own ideas letting them develop and contribute to the advance of mankind.

But occasionally that book with new ideas and new approaches does come along, and is all the more to be treasured for its rarity.

Such a book is Gary Hoppenstand's *In Search of the Paper Tiger*. Hoppenstand approached the idea of the book in the proper way—that of the skeptic who said that not all the great ideas about popular culture have been covered in the books of his predecessors. He felt that all those books, useful to him as they had been, needed revisions, new and updated editions, or that we need new studies that will supplement and might replace them. With these ideas in mind, and with the truly searching and iconoclastic nature, he set out to see how he could add one useful rung in the ladder of scholarship.

And he has accomplished his goal. His study of the sociological side of the humanities in popular culture is a new and useful approach. Hoppenstand has managed to cross the line of contempt and disdain that many scholars, even well-informed humanities scholars, hold for the social sciences. He has recognized that these sciences have a great deal to contribute to the study of the humanities, just as, hopefully, the humanities have much to contribute to the study of the social sciences.

Hoppenstand's book is, thus, not only a step up but also a step across. As such it accomplishes a great deal, and will be critical in its contribution to all people interested in the humanities and popular culture.

Ray B. Browne

FOREWORD
The Eye of the Tiger

THE SOCIAL-PSYCHOLOGICAL PRACTICE of world construction entails a continual cognitive labor. In an effort to place mental identification "tags" on the objects, the life-experience sequences and the emotions that comprise the fundamental touchstones of the human experience, man catalogues his life. He rationally defines those discrete aspects of a potentially hostile environment that assist him in survival, such as food, clothing and shelter, and communicates his knowledge to peer group members so that others of his kind can survive and contribute to a community well-being. If any portion of this world construction dialogue breaks down—a food source not defined as safe or poisonous, the locales of a food source not properly cultivated, the knowledge of food gathering and distribution techniques not effectively disclosed to community members—then personal survival is in jeopardy. Yet, even when the particulars of the definitions of survival are recognized, recorded and distributed, the certainty of that survival remains in doubt. Planted crops fail because of drought or flood. Vermin and disease attack stored grain. War counterbalances civic progress. Man is indeed a cataloguer of survival, but he is an eminently suspicious cataloguer. It is not enough for him to know about survival. He must also know about the *quality* of survival, which crop grows best in what conditions, which storage method protects the grain best, what political system best protects the community from potential invaders. Thus, man as creator of his culture and the artifacts of that culture persists in supporting a paradigm that esthetically ranks the objects of his creation.

As human cultures became tied to the land on which they farmed, depending less on a hunting/gathering nomadic lifestyle, property and possessions assumed greater value within the community, engendering institutional systems which allowed definitions of

1

ownership. Wealth could be more easily accumulated within permanent communities since one did not have to worry about transporting it around, as did, for example, nomadic groups when they moved in search of food. The permanency of land ownership and the cognitive attachment of wealth to that land created new problems, however. How do those who "own" the land (and the possessions of the land) retain ownership, protecting their claims from hostile others and insuring the perpetuation of their legacy to their offspring? Political power presented a solution to this problem. With the definition of wealth and the ability to inventory wealth, and with evolving socio-political structures that protected and distributed wealth, social rank within a community quickly became equated with possessions—the ability to protect one's holdings and the ability to wrest a rival's holdings. The parameters of political power resided with those who possessed the most land, the most gold and the most warriors. The power-elite of the community, with the resource of wealth (i.e. those possessions that best insure survival) as a device to insure the support and protection of fellow members, with the sanctioned authority to impose their will upon fellow members, possessed the ability to structure the division of labor, work required to insure the stability of food production and defense. Consequently, those who possessed the least were delegated the most laborious and menial chores while those who possessed the most directed the efforts of others. As the power-elite became freed from the time-consuming tasks now performed by their social inferiors, their attentions diverted to activities that would enhance the enjoyment of their leisure time.

Symbolic communication systems proved invaluable in determining the success factor of man's potential to survive. Stylized illustration (as symbolic communication or language), for example, provided a means by which events could be permanently charted and recorded, and consequently would not be suspect to the haphazard variants of oral information. Language not only expressed in an economical fashion the particulars of survival, it also assisted in the definition of the self, the community and the cosmos. A catalog of life was impossible without a consensus understanding of the mental "building blocks" needed to structure the life experience. Yet, man, as the suspicious cataloguer, was driven to develop the superior illustration—one that better represented the object or sequence of significant events—the more effective language.

The widening of the gap between the powerful and the powerless in a community eventually caused the time-consuming tasks required for survival to be delegated to an increasingly possessionless work force, and with a relatively small power-elite dominating the wealth of the community and being afforded increasing amounts of leisure time, the power-elite's social application of symbolic communication systems towards an enhancement of their leisure time became commonplace. Craftsmen of symbolic communication were nurtured and employed by the power-elite to devise methods by which objects could be graphically enhanced. The homes of the rich and powerful became targets of architectural embroidery. Centers of worship, run by the powerful, as well, received the attention of the employed craftsman. Illustration evolved into sculpture and graphic illustration, and was often utilized by the power-elite to preserve the image of important class members or meaningful social events. These craftsmen of symbolic communication vied with one another for the attention of the power-elite (and the limited wealth resources of the power-elite). Quality of illustration and language, or the subjectively interpreted *art* of communication, consequently became the standard of judgement and the coin of survival for the craftsman. Ultimately, the craft of symbolic communication transformed into the art of symbols, and the art of symbols, as standardizations became formularized, transfigured into "fine" art.

In order to insure the continuance of wealth and social supremacy over time, the community's power-elite framed systems of power dispersal and endowments, usually revolving around the nuclear and extended family (or pseudo-family/religious) structures, and as a particular community advanced towards a more complex and sophisticated social design, notably in the areas of Africa, Asia, the Middle East and the Mediterranean Sea several thousand years before the birth of Christ and in Western Europe after the political decline of the Roman Empire several hundred years after the birth of Christ, occupation and status were equated. Delegation of authority entrenched itself as the profession of the noble family or the state church (manifestations of the power-elite), and as authority decisions became more varied and time-consuming for the nobility, the role of esthetically determining the superior art forms of the rich and powerful was further delegated to the art critic, an educated specialist of sorts who established standards of quality and acceptance for and by the nobility. Art, then, further divorced and isolated itself from the broad cultural flow of the peasant classes, and was additionally appropriated by an ever narrowing social class. The application for ritual and formula stylized artistic expression totally within a subjective criterion established by the art critic. Since it was crucial that the art critic legitimize the value of his opinions in the minds of the nobility (so that the art critic's economic security would be insured), the notion of "country-club" art—or fine art—became prominent. Conventions of artistic expression were formed that demanded high social status, specialized training or great wealth. Without these keys to membership in the fine arts country club, participation by the general population was impossible.

With the advent of the Industrial Revolution: with the invention of the printing press, the high-speed steam printing press, the electronic teat that fed the newly-birthed children of pulpwood paper, film, radio, vinal record and television; with the increase in numbers of people, numbers of cities, machines that infused both money and leisure time into those segments of the population who never possessed such luxuries; with an increase in education that dramatically affected a widening population base; with evolving giant economic speculators who invested the increasing quantities of capital in products that fed the leisure time desires of the working classes, and, of course, drained both the money and the time of those working classes in the name of entertainment—the world of art and artist and critic became an unwitting casualty of the revolution. The Industrial Revolution was a social and artistic revolution as well.

No longer did entertainment strictly apply to the wealthy, the powerful, the educated. For the first time in human history, nearly *all* social classes could find a diversion from their work for as little or as much money as their pockets held. But interestingly, fine art and the critics of fine art, resurrected themselves from their social graves and adapted to the changing demands of the revolution. In an effort to maintain a measure of control over the intellectual artistic community (and to preserve their function as employed evaluators), the post-industrial fine art critic devised methods by which the standards of specialized education, high social status and wealth could be re-applied to the definition of art. The simplest and most practical solution to establishing a new definition of art was to delineate a substantive difference between fine art *per se* and the entertainment by-product of the Industrial Revolution, mass media art. Thus, the fine art critic engendered a paradigm that supported the contention that entertainment forms birthed by the mass media were inferior, sub-standard, created by and for a vast mob of intellectual morons, a mob possessing little or no esthetic standards of entertainment. Personal artistic expression became highly valued; mass expression became condemned. The fine art critic invented (or re-used) discrete languages of evaluation that divorced artistic expression from mass participation. Isolated art institutions were cultivated by the fine art critic, such as the art museum, the salon and the university, where access was restricted to the general public. Support of the fine arts, including the financial support of artists operating within the paradigm of personal, stylized, highly subjective expression, was monopolized by the power-elite (under the guidance of the fine art critic) demonstrating a type of social status.

Print media entertainment, over time, underwent what can be termed a cycle of social acceptance that further led to artistic acceptance by the fine art critic. This cycle possessed four stages: 1) technological advancement of the mass media entertainment form; 2) social and artistic rejection of the form; 3) expansion and continued prosperity of the form, despite social and artistic rejection; and 4) social and artistic acceptance of the form fostered by its healthy persistence over time. Detective fiction, specifically the hard-boiled tradition that flourished in the American pulp magazines of the 1920s and 1930s, offers an excellent example of this process.

Initially, the pulp magazines evolved from the ashes of the dime novel industry, burgeoning into a print empire of genres, including fantasy, science fiction, Western, adventure, romance and detective fiction. Though these numerous publications achieved tremendous popularity among a mass readership, the literary art critic, sensing that the bastions of literature were being threatened by this pulp menace, leveled arguments against the violent and sexual content—and most importantly, the so-called sub-literary style—of the pulps, arguments that could just as easily have been applied to the Hemingways and the Faulkners of the time. Print technological advancements made the pulp magazine readily available to the masses, and what was really an issue here was social class. Cultural and language barriers were torn down since a highly refined taste mind-set was unnecessary for understanding this new print medium. Social status, and more importantly wealth, were demolished as prerequisites for participation since payment for entertainment reading was well within the means of a large working class audience. But as the working class embraced this new inexpensive entertainment, the middle and upper classes became more suspicious, indeed, threatened, of this fiction industry, leading to claims of subversion of morality, which brings us to the second stage of the media cycle.

As the middle and upper classes discovered what the working

class was reading in the backs of those drugstore storerooms, they reacted as would a matron aunt when catching her rebellious nephew smoking a cigarette behind her back. Dashiell Hammett and his following of hard-boiled writers were, at best, looked down upon as being merely "pulp" (a demeaning term meaning inferior which still is used today), and were, at worst, seen as endangering the minds of the young, the working and immigrant classes. The language of the hard-boiled story was of the street, not the parlor. The social invention of the new "hard-boiled pulp magazine language," a language that middle and upper class caretakers and disseminators had no influence over and which permitted a culturally deprived social class the capacity to involve themselves in a leisure time activity (previously the guarded domain of the power-elite), forced the politics of social power to realign. Social and critical rejection of any evolving new media form, like the hard-boiled pulp story, is not a moral issue, but a political issue. Morality was, and is, an implement employed by the directors of a social group to maintain the foundation of a power structure that maintains the status quo. Technological revolution, the power-elite recognizes, translates into social revolution, and the most effective method to combat the entrenchment of new media technologies is to club the mass audience with a powerful, traditional moral argument. The question of morality was a force of suppression in the early years of the pulp magazine industry, but as with any application of force, the resistance to that force increases diametrically as the force itself increases. With hard-boiled pulp fiction, as the audience widened, resisting numerous attempts to restrict and censor content and audience participation, the technological/social revolution solidified, forcing the members of the middle and upper classes to re-evaluate their political position. Sin, as anti-fiction apologia, simply failed to be an effective suppressant of the medium.

Thus, regardless of the concentrated efforts of the middle class to over-regulate—and even suppress—the activities of working class participation with popular literary formulas, the business of the pulp magazines persisted, flourishing. The continued stamina of hard-boiled pulp entertainment despite the strongest sanctions of the social and moral critics illustrated several points. First, as with any new media form, the technological novelty of that form fosters an audience fascination which initially guarantees commercial success. Second, moral arguments leveled against the content of hard-boiled pulp fiction denies the mass audience its concern with issues of sex and violence. If the pulps were a new language, a language that required little or no special education or status privileges for participation, then the particulars, or grammar, of the language would necessarily involve life issues, which possess universal concerns, like sex and violence. Attacking these powerful life issues involved denying the very humanness of the human condition.

The middle and upper classes, recognizing that their best attempts to stifle a medium and a formula that could not be stifled, and recognizing that the novelty of the hard-boiled story was a powerful attraction to their own socio-political interests, began incorporating the medium/formula, adopting it as their own entertainment. This process not only helps to diffuse the political danger of working class participation at the exclusion of other social groups, it allows the dominant social groups the ability to control the subject matter of fiction and the dynamics of its distribution. In other words, if you can't beat them, have them join you. Being "banned in Boston" (as were James M. Cain's novels) was no longer a bad thing, but instead was a measure of "quality."

Which brings us to the fourth and final aspect of the media cycle: as the new medium is ultimately recognized and accepted by the power-elite, that form is culturally dissected by the agents of the power-elite (the fine art critic, for example), so that social divisions are reinforced. With hard-boiled fiction, then, Hammett's, Chandler's and Cain's work became valued as superior examples of fiction, being termed (as they have been) examples of a new American "art" form by the literary critic. But as this fiction has been elevated to its artistic pedestal, new popular formula victims have taken its place, like the paperback vigilante hero (the Executioner, for example), and the cycle begins anew.

The earliest artistic casualty of the mass media revolution during the mid-nineteenth century in America was fiction. Prior to Beadle and Adams' major contribution to the print medium, the dime novel, in 1860, the intellectual hierarchy was given an earth-resounding shake. The book business pre-1860 was essentially a "cottage" industry. Authors were members of the upper social and economic classes, and they often financed the printing, through local bookstores (which during that era served double duty as publishers and booksellers), of their own work. Their print runs were relatively small, the costs of the books high, and their distribution miniscule. Only the wealthy intelligentsia of the Boston/New York/Philadelphia "tea-cup" societies posssessed the means to participate in the literary experience, and thus early, pre-dime novel fiction tended to be introspective, highbrow and politically illustrative of the upper social classes. The entrepreneurial invention of the dime novel, combined with the expansion of an educated middle class engendered by the Industrial Revolution, tore fiction away from the East Coast intelligentsia and deposited it squarely upon the shoulders of a widespread American populace, eager to be entertained. The emphasis of fiction became commercial, rather than artistic, as expanding publishing empires vied with one another for a larger piece of the economic publishing pie. The cottage industry quickly re-formed into profitable concerns and has remained at this stage to the present. The threat of mass mediated fiction soon became evident to the American power-elite. The cognitive effort of reading generates original thought that perhaps is contradictory to the vested interests of the socially powerful. Popular fiction underwent its own version of the media cycle, stages of initial rejection and grudging acceptance, with the subjective artistic/moral argument constantly being leveled against it. Artistic evaluation was the smoking gun, the fine art critic the red-handed killer and popular print mass media the potential victim.

In recent years, there has been a general recognition in the critical and academic communities of the potential value of objective analysis of popular, mass mediated story formulas, perhaps spearheaded by the efforts of the myth/symbol school of literary criticism. With the publication of Henry Nash Smith's study of the American frontier experience, *The Virgin Land* (and his examination of the American frontier dime novel as literary object), through the publication of John Cawelti's survey of popular formulas, *Adventure, Mystery, and Romance*, a grudging awareness has grown of the social and cultural influence of the mass entertainment experience. But this grudging awareness has been tempered, and even blunted, by the traditional bugaboos of artistic quality, of literary merit and ultimately, social value. The scholar, the academic and the fine art critic need to perceive that a new methodology is required to address the larger social questions of fiction, in particular popular fiction. They need to recognize that traditional literary criticism is a socially created device that subjectively interprets issues of quality and value, issues that are meaningless when confronted with mass media print entertainment forms. Social, rather than artistic, processes are the dynamic matrix of the literary experience, since popular fiction is a socially engendered product of a collective social experience, and the artistic question is a politically self-serving device that enforces status, social power and prestige.

This study, consequently, presents an argument against evaluation. It suggests that the tools of the literary critic need to be re-worked, or re-defined if you will, so that the process of social life (rather than the product of personal expression) and the relationship of the popular story form to that process can better be interpreted.

The extended metaphor of the following social-psychological examination of myth, popular formula and the mystery genre is the tiger, that most remarkable creature of perception. Tigers can be viewed any numbers of ways. For the deer, tigers are engines of violent death, yet for the tiger, hunting and killing are merely the means of survival, of living. For the poet or illustrator, tigers are beautifully symmetrical animals, possessing grace, form, color and enigma. For the zoologist, they are a class of predators functioning according to the designs of nature within a particular ecological environment. Death, life, poetic enigma and natural function: all of these concepts define the same thing, contradicting each other yet not being contradictory.

Like the tiger, the mystery genre can be many things: stories of life, stories of death, tales of human destruction and human triumph, simple leisure entertainment and complex socializer. The first chapter of this study will present social construction of reality theory as a methodology upon which the structure of mass mediated popular fiction can be examined, with definitions of myth and formula postulated, and a new language of literary analysis advanced that acknowledges the socially defining, democratizing experience of popular fiction. The second chapter narrows the focus of social-psychological analysis to the mystery genre, while the balance of chapters examines the taxonomy of this genre, employing seminal or most representative mystery stories as the basis for a sociological/ literary exploration of the dynamic interaction between the individual and his society. An understanding of social perception is the thread that connects the tiger and the mystery. No one in his right mind would ever suggest that tigers and fiction are similar, but they are. After all, it is merely a matter of perception.

Gary Hoppenstand
1986

CHAPTER I

Defining the Paper Tiger:
A Social Psychological Perspective
of the Identity of Myth and Popular
Literary Formulas

The Birth of the Paper Tiger

THE ABILITY OF THE INDIVIDUAL to effectively describe those things of his social being which are meaningful is useful as a mechanism of survival. The individual is a consummate social storyteller, and the stories of his community, his past and future assist him with his day to day struggle with life. The story parallels the life experience. Its powerful message describes both individual conflicts with hostile forces and, indeed, with issues that elaborate significant global concerns. The individual's storytelling ability *is* a metaphor of learning. The story is a communication device that both entertains and educates the listener (or reader) and the teller. It ritualizes the unknown into understandable concepts, and it conceptualizes the understandable into predictable patterns of action. It focuses thought, illustrates history and defines wishes and aspirations. It is the door to heaven, the apology of hell. It is the tool by which he hammers the specter of his own morality. It is the anvil of his being. The singular ability of a particular story to unite common experience for a social group, despite the plurality of individualism, suggests that the more basic the story's plot, the more predictable its message, the more fundamental the story's characters—then, the more successful its function. Though its birth was probably coeval with the first social intercourse between two individuals, the advent of the Industrial Revolution and mass media in Europe and America offered the perfect vehicle for the story. Technology stylized storytelling, systematized it and granted it the widest audience base possible. Technology preserved a storytelling cultural history of the way things should have been and the way things

11

will be. And foremost, above anything else, technological storytelling entertained because it simply and effectively said "life is knowable; death can be defeated; existence is stable." The foundation of the popular story is myth. The technological device of mass media is the structural shell of mythmaking. Thus, an effective methodology for the examination of the myth foundation of the popular story and the structure of technological mythmaking is the myth/symbol approach, though this methodology is not without its drawbacks.

The myth/symbol school of literary criticism recognizes the crucial relationship between story and myth-narrative, but this school's collective explanations of subsequent socialization processes rely much too heavily upon the products of myth narrative. When R.W.B. Lewis, for example, states in the introduction to his book *The American Adam* that he is primarily concerned with the various symbols that led to the formation of an American myth—with the history of ideas and representative imagery that expresses an artistic sort of national paradigm or mind-set—he is actually basing this paradigm upon the products of a narrow, aristocratic intellectual and literary intelligentsia that flourished in America during the latter part of the 18th and the early decades of the 19th centuries. Lewis advocates his position by suggesting that his view of myth concerns the history of ideas, unrelated to sociology or anthropology, and that his interest is therefore limited to articulate thinkers and conscious artists.[1] Lewis is actually contributing to the construction of a rigid intellectual consciousness, a consciousness that fails to recognize the limitations of advocating a monomythic vision, a consciousness that elevates and deliberately mystifies a cognitively shaky tunnel view of American history. Lewis' particular myth/symbol approach ultimately functions as a fiction itself, heavily clothed by the illusion of highly selective facts, a nicely tailored suit, attractive in its cut, but nonetheless cut of cheap cloth and sewn with weak thread. Divorcing the *product* of myth from the *process* of myth creates a garment destined to fall apart.

Lewis was not the first literary historian or art critic to fit a fiction upon the outline of an American "experience," and then fail to recognize the invented craft of his own fiction. Frederick Jackson Turner formulated a rationale, equally rigid, in his essay/lecture "The Significance of the Frontier in American History," in which he described a "unique" American happening, the frontier experience, in which the existence of an area of free land, its continuous recession, and the advance of American settlement westward, explain American development.[2] Turner plays down the process of myth and isolates its product. Thus, according to Turner, American thought, indeed its very national character, is illustrated by its frontier heritage. Turner's Frontier Thesis, presented at the American Historical Association meeting at the 1893 Chicago World's Fair, quickly founded an academic following devoted to the lavish monomythic interpretation of American history. But such easily bandied concepts as "free land" tend to legitimize an invented causal relationship without sociologically understanding the process of that legitimization. Turner and his followers comprehend only half of the nature of myth.

The "father" of the literary myth/symbol approach, Henry Nash Smith, adopting Turner's Frontier Thesis, for example, prefaces his survey of American frontier history and literature, *Virgin Land*, with a vague delineation of what myths and symbols are, briefly suggesting in his introduction that myths are "intellectual constructions that fuse concept and emotion into an image."[3] Smith's definition exhibits two major problems. First, in stating that myths and symbols are an intellectual construct—though recognizing that myths are collective representations—without delivering a theoretical basis upon which myths and symbols are created, Smith has denied us an understanding of the complex social psychological processes inherent in the social frame of the creation of an image. Second, with Smith's claim that myths exist on a "different plane" of social interactionism, he implies that myths hold some sort of valid empiricism that defies objective critical examination. Myths do not exist on any theoretical plane outside socio-economic ideology. They function as a tool of that ideology's own legitimized creation.

Perhaps the most thorough of the myth/symbolists, Richard Slotkin, recognizes the role sociology plays in the mythgenesis process, claiming that "myth-making is simultaneously a psychological and a social activity."[4] And thus, in his massive study *Regeneration Through Violence: The Mythology of the American Frontier, 1600-1860*, he devotes an entire chapter to an explication of the origins of myth and myth-narrative. Slotkin presents mythology as a complex of narratives that dramatizes a world vision of a culture or a group of people. He claims that myth-narratives recapitulate a peoples' experience with their land and with their gods, and, in addition, he maintains that the ultimate source of myth derives from the human mind.[5] Slotkin's analysis of myth hits closest to the sociological heart of mythgenesis. However, when Slotkin illustrates the relationship of the individual to his myth-narratives, without addressing the social role that language plays in the establishment of the individual's definitions of reality, then he displays a profound ignorance of mythgenesis and of resulting myth-narratives. Myth, as we shall see later in this chapter, is, after all, the extended representation of a language system, and as language defines such things as objects, other individuals and cultural paradigms, so too does it place the individual in an institutional order.

The myth/symbol scholars have fallen into a narcissism trap, resulting from several crucial, incorrect assumptions. First, by not providing a detailed elaboration of the process of the sociology of knowledge, any analysis of myth becomes decontextualized and meaningless. Second, the non-recognition of the importance of language in the development of society (and subsequent manipulations of that society) basically ignores the single most important ingredient of social awareness. Third, the related beliefs of discriminatory myth analysis and presentism can color cultural inquiry to such an extent as to render it intellectually harmful.

What these three, and successive myth/symbol critics, fail to acknowledge is the paradox of myth. Myth indeed is an intellectual construct, but it is a construct that incrementally invents, out of a free-floating chaos of untold particles of potentially meaningless data, a society. Myth does not deny the contributions of articulate thinkers and conscious artists, but it is primarily fabricated of story forms written by the mass artist, who has in the past been incorrectly labelled by literary critics as merely "pot-boiling" formula fiction to please unartistic popular taste. Myth embodies psychological and social processes, but it denies by its very nature the simplicity of paradigm and favors the complexity of multiple function.

To understand the essence of this paradox better, we must begin with an understanding of the socialization process itself. The device of this understanding resides with social psychology, specifically the sociology of knowledge. Peter L. Berger and Thomas Luckmann suggest in *The Social Construction of Reality* (1966) that the phenomenon known as the sociology of knowledge must center upon the dynamic relationship between the individual, society and the process of gathering information, of observing one's physical environment and cognitively codifying that environment into patterns of living: in other words, comprehending what a society perceives of as being important to its survival. Regarding the design of human knowledge, including socialization and education, the sociology of knowledge endeavors to comprehend the creation of thought, and by uncovering the skin of man's presupposed notions of existence, it seeks to establish a theoretical basis for cultural inquiry. The sociology of knowledge is concerned with man's social construction of reality.[6]

The core notion of the sociology of knowledge fixes on human thought and the social context within which it arises.[7] Since mythmaking, and the popular story that affect and reflect it, is primarily a product of thought, the focus of any analysis of mythgenesis should necessarily bear witness to the *process* of myth. Popular formula fiction is a tool of this process, and an examination of formula discloses a social psychological skeleton upon which is fleshed that assembly of genres, formulas and motifs comprising our tiger, which we call "modern European/Anglo-American mass-mediated print fiction."

Myth constitutes a powerful element of man's invention of the world. Peter L. Berger, in his book *The Sacred Canopy* (1967), illustrates the workings of the social construction of reality. Berger suggests that the whole of society, including each discrete aspect of that whole, such as the products of individual and group thought, is a human creation, possessing no other origin than what is given to it by man. But once created by man, society affects its producer. There can be no society without the human mind to create it and human activity to sustain it. In addition, there can be no society without the individual. Via this dialectic relationship, the individual is cognitively created by society: its norms, its history, its cultural products; and in turn the individual produces society. Berger claims that each person is a biography within the larger story of the social group. It precedes the birth of the individual and it will survive the individual's death. Society writes the biography of the individual, transforming him into a social member, granting an identity and providing the tasks that comprise the individual's existence. The person cannot exist apart from his world.[8]

Myth, as an expression of society, and popular literary formula, as an expression of myth, not only are intellectual by-products of the socialization process, they are the means of socialization themselves. The myth-narrative that recounts nationalistic origins (or the popular high-fantasy heroic quest tale that mirrors a sub-unit of the myth-narrative), is invented by the individual and society and subsequently re-acts to the invention of time. The individual places himself within a cultural context, acts with the product of that context (myth and popular stories) and is affected. Variations of myth-narrative arise when new stimuli are introduced into the culture, and refinements of story are performed. Thus, popular stories serve as a textbook of social norms and expectations, demanding consideration of a collective type. Without the myth, without the popular story, identity is lost and alienation occurs.

The *process* of myth, then perhaps more than the *product* of myth, becomes significant as a means of societal inquiry. Berger states that the process of social interaction is comprised of three moments or steps. Berger identifies these as externalization, objectivation and internalization, and suggests that only if these three moments are understood together can an empirically valid view of society be maintained. Externalization, Berger says, is the ongoing outpouring of human being into the world, both in the physical and mental activity of the individual. Objectivation, he continues, is the attainment by the products of this activity (again both physical and mental) of a reality that confronts its original producers as a facticity external to and other than themselves. Internalization, he concludes, is the reappropriation by people of this same reality, transforming it once again from the structures of the objective world into the structures of the subjective consciousness.[9] Through the process of externalization, myth is invented as a by-product of society, and the popular story as a by-product of myth. Through the process of objectivation, the mass media artifacts that transmit myth and popular stories are produced, and it is through internalization that mass media artifacts in turn reform myth and story, acting as a catalyst of further human activity at the individual and group levels, both consciously and subconsciously.

Berger's methodology can be employed to dispute the paradigmatic inflexibility of the myth/symbolists' analysis of myth and fiction. Society, as Berger tells us, as objective reality, provides a world for the individual to inhabit. This social world collectively encompasses the biography of the individual, which during the life of the individual is unearthed as a series of events within the natural, cultural and historical world. Berger claims that the individual's own biography is objectively real only in as much as it may be understood within the important structures of the social world. The individual may possess a wide range of personal interpretations about his environment, but these personal interpretations nonetheless are framed by an objective, collective reference.[10] Myths and popular stories are universal structures within which their participants identify and locate their own life experiences. They are responsive to the give and take of the individual. The classical detective story, though relatively rigid in formula, can offer a variety of reader responses. The frame is defined by boundaries, and a collection of these frames is incorporated in the larger frame of myth-narrative. Variants of experience are allowed, but the conventions of the story structure restrict too radical a reading. A multiplicity of worldviews exist, yet collectively these worldviews suggest a recognizable pattern.

Popular fiction possesses a history that dates back to Western industrial and democratic revolutions, and even further back in oral, tradition-based culture. Berger claims that every society that exists over a period of time encounters the dilemma of transmitting knowledge and custom from one generation to the next. This dilemma can be attacked, Berger says, by means of socialization: the process by which a new generation is taught to live in accordance with the institutional programs of society.[11] Socialization encompasses the history of society and facilitates this transmission of history. Fiction, as agent of the socialization process, instructs new social members in its conventions (or traditions—a better word choice). Ultimately, the question that should be raised by the literary critic or sociologist is: "What lessons are taught?" Refining the essence of popular fiction to its most basic compounds, two archetypal concerns appear: life (i.e. sex and the birth experience) and death.

All the varieties of popular formula fiction primarily deal with issues of life and death. Fiction's basic constitution is comprised of conflict, and the most basic of conflicts is life against death. This conflict provides the outermost frame of the socialization process, which then becomes a collective issue via the technomic function of mass media. If myth, as the larger receptacle of popular fiction, as the invention of the individual, as the affector of the individual's action, *is* a socially constructed reality, then the constant of that reality is the death crisis. Myth and fiction function as educators of survival.

For our purposes, we can employ Peter Berger's and Thomas Luckmann's sociological definition of the term "mythology," which presents us with an empirical footing that eludes the highly subjective, traditional myth/symbol approach. Mythology, Berger and Luckmann state, maintains the conception of the universe and provides methods of legitimization for support. Mythology necessarily arises in the development of human thought and is contextualized by history over time. The oldest forms of legitimization are mythological. As Berger and Luckmann define it, mythology is a conception of reality that presents the everyday world as being affected by sacred forces. There results a correlation between the social and the cosmic, which binds reality into a single creation.[12] Basically, mythology is concerned with explanations. It answers questions about the context of life, the past, present and future, and about death. What results is a dialectic between the changing and the unchanging, between the process of the social construction of reality and the certainty of physical death (a human archetypal issue) and this results in paradox. Myth and popular formula fiction are documents of this paradox. We have a tiger (a paper tiger, if you will) by the tail, and this tiger, defined by myth/symbolists as paradigm and by the sociologists as reality construction, is a bit of both. But, after all, myth (and the conglomerate of popular literary formulas included within myth-narrative structures) is only a paper tiger and paper tigers do not bite. They do, however, warrant investigation.

The Form of the Paper Tiger

Formula—one of the leading literary devices on which myth is employed—is one of those words that encompass a whole range of meanings and interpretations, and which, for our purposes, needs to be fully defined before we undertake a taxonomy of contemporary popular European/American print story forms. One of the most comprehensive recent attempts to strike at the heart of the makeup of popular formulas is John G. Cawelti's *Adventure, Mystery and Romance,* so we will begin our study by briefly illustrating the strengths and weaknesses of Cawelti's argument. Further, the specifics of formula and formula construction will be advanced which emphasize the social-psychological and psycho-linguistic functions of the phenomenon of popular storytelling. And, third, a general overview of the mystery genre will be postulated that will serve as a frame for a more detailed discussion of the formulas and sub-formulas in that genre.

Cawelti's definition of formula centers on two points: the art of formula and the cultural dynamics of formula. Cawelti argues that, primarily, formula literature is a kind of literary art, and thus it can be analyzed and evaluated like any other kind of literature.[13] He suggests that formula is composed of two properties. The first property, which he terms standardization or convention, is the essence of all literature. These conventions establish a common ground between writers and audiences, and they reflect the interests of audiences, creators and distributors.[14] Arguing that audiences find emotional satisfaction and security in a familiar form, Cawelti states that the audiences' experiences with a formula gives them a sense of what to expect in new individual examples, thereby increasing the capacity for understanding and enjoying the details of a work. Conventions speed the writing of formula fiction, since the writer—once familiar with the outlines of the formula—does not have to make as many difficult artistic decisions as other novelists, and they establish audience pleasure by forming a world that depends on its intensification of a familiar experience.[15] And yet, Cawelti states, all good formulaic writers need at least two special artistic skills: the ability to give new vitality to stereotypes and the capacity to invent new touches of plot or setting that are still within the formulaic limits.[16] These skills, which Cawelti identifies as invention, need to be effectively balanced with literary conventions in order both to preserve the integrity of the emotional security that formulas provide and to foster new story directions so that formulas do not become stale and redundant.

The cultural dynamics of formula, Cawelti tells us, are composed in part by the dominant influence of the goals of escape and entertainment. The artistry of escape in formulas necessarily stresses intense and immediate kinds of excitement and gratification. The more satisfying form of escape, Cawelti suggests, is one that can sustain itself over a longer period of time and arrive at some sense of completion and fulfillment within itself.[17] Formula also recognizes two different psychological needs, both of which play an important part in shaping the kind of imaginative experiences we pursue for relaxation and regeneration. Cawelti says that, first of all, we seek moments of intense excitement and interest in order to get away from the boredom and ennui that are particularly prevalent in the relatively secure, routine and organized lives of the great majority of the contemporary American and Western European public. While, at the same time, we seek escape from our consciousness of the ultimate insecurities and ambiguities that afflict even the most secure sort of life: death, the failure of love, our inability to accomplish all we had hoped for, the threat of atomic holocaust.[18] Formulas, Cawelti informs us, are cultural products and in turn presumably have some sort of influence on culture because they become conventional ways of representing and relating certain images, symbols, themes and myths.[19] Arguing from Henry Nash Smith's myth/symbol approach, Cawelti postulates that the work of art, including formula fiction, consists of a complex of symbols or myths that are imaginative orderings of experience. These symbols or myths are defined as images or patterns of images charged with a variety of feelings and meanings and they become, therefore, modes of perception as well as simple reflections of reality.[20] Cawelti advances an interrelated hypotheses about the dialectic between formulaic literature and the culture that produces and enjoys it. First, he says that formula stories affirm existing interests and attitudes by presenting an imaginary world that is aligned with these interests and attitudes. Second, formulas resolve tensions and ambiguities resulting from the conflicting interests of different groups within the culture or from ambiguous attitudes toward particular values. Third, formulas enable the audience to explore in fantasy the boundary between the permitted and the forbidden and to experience in a carefully controlled way the possibility of stepping across this boundary. And, fourth, literary formulas assist in the process of assimilating changes in values to traditional imaginative constructs.[21]

Though Cawelti is essentially correct in his analysis of formula construction and formula function in society, he fails to explore the particulars of that construction or process of that function in any meaningful way. If formula requires a balance of convention and invention in order to be artistically successful, how is this accomplished? If formula provides emotional excitement, gratification and security, how is this done? And if formula reflects its audience and helps shape its perceptions, what are the specifics of this social process? Cawelti's methodology needs to be fleshed-out, filled-in and further clarified in order to be meaningful. He has done half a job; he has proposed half of an argument and we must complete his task.

In order to understand better the process between formula writing and formula reading and the relationship between the affecting and reflecting values of formula in society, two theories prove valuable, and they are social psychology and psycho-linguistics. As argued earlier, myth making and formula construction (as a specific example of myth-making) are representative elements of the social construction of reality. All human societies, as Peter L. Berger suggests, are enterprises in world building.[22] Formula construction is an integral part of this world building, and it is important that it be understood in terms of a dialectic process. Formula is a product of society that in turn affects society. As a person gains identity within society, formula fiction assists the individual's attainment of that identity. Formula is a social tool that provides stability and direction. The convention of formula that Cawelti identifies is used to provide cultural foundations. Ultimately, society controls and directs the actions of the individual, and formula is a means by which society imposes its objective reality. Formula is a method of social control, prescribing punishment for aberrant individuals. The harsh justice of an avenger-detective figure in formula detective fiction thus becomes better understood in these terms, as do the graphic depictions of horror fiction (as individuals who defy taboo are subsequently treated to all manner of harsh supernatural retribution). The effectiveness of a society's sanctions on individual conduct is a demonstration of the validity of its reality. Formula fiction, then, is not fantasy or escapism, but an active and effective method for maintaining the mechanisms of social control. It is, in part, a process by which reality is imposed upon members of society.

Formula fiction is first and foremost a language system. Language is the product of human invention over time. Formulaic stories, as a specific development of the English language, possess an objective reality for their readers with prescribed texts for human action. These stories are vehicles for discourse and understanding of mores and norms, and of the natural world. They offer ready-made niches for the individual to inhabit.

The development of popular mass-mediated formula fiction as an articulation of a language system which communicates a complex of expressions, social relationships and taboos suggests a type of hierarchal structure. Claude Levi-Strauss defines the value of a structural approach to the study of culture, particularly employing linguistics as a methodology:

Linguistics occupies a special place among the social sciences, to whose ranks it unquestionably belongs. It is not merely a social science like the others, but, rather, the one in which by far the greatest progress has been made. It is probably the only one which can truly claim to be a science and which has achieved both the formulation of an empirical method and an understanding of the nature of the data submitted to its analysis.[23]

And thus, so that we better understand the function of formula fiction as a language that defines reality, and that transmits knowledge over space and time, an examination into the chemistry of structuralism, in particular the psycho-linguistic relationship between formula writing and formula reading, is useful.

Psycho-linguistics, as Frank Smith defines it, "is the process of reading that translates print into meaningful cognitive understanding."[24] Reading is most effective, Smith claims, when a contextual frame is imposed upon the content. It is not effective as an exercise in decoding words and phrases.[25] Reading is an active process, not a passive one, thus the greater amount of information and knowledge the reader can bring to the text, the greater the meaning the reader derives and the less dependent the reader is upon visual information.[26] Formula fiction provides the ability for active reader participation since it is part of the socialization process that defines reality. By its conventional nature, formula fiction reduces social uncertainty as it offers a predictable story frame, and because of the redundancy of story motifs in formula fiction, it effectively incorporates prior reader knowledge that facilitates the communication of that knowledge.

Smith claims that readers do not normally attend to print with blank minds, with no prior purpose and with no expectation of what they might find in the text. By not bringing to print a narrow set of expectations, but rather a wide range of possible expectations, readers can overcome many difficulties in deriving information from text. Readers search for those elements that are meaningful to them. Reading comprehension, Smith informs us, is not a matter of putting names to nonsense and struggling to make sense of the result, but of operating in the realm of meaningfulness all the time.[27] Formula fiction provides an example of how readers use their language to foretell social meaning and to enhance the success of information-processing. Thus, formula fiction establishes a direct line of communication of social information and expectations between writer and reader, between fiction and society. It might be said, Smith argues, that a book is comprehended (from the writer's point of view, at least) when the reader's predictions mirror the writer's intentions at all levels,[28] and formula fiction is one important aspect of writing as an intentional manipulation of the reader's predictions.

Having defined the role that formula fiction plays in the social construction of reality and in the psycho-linguistic manipulation of print into meaningful predictions of socialization and communication, we need to address the specific language of formula: what exactly constitutes formula? What is its structure and how does this structure bind the story into a comprehensible hierarchy of social prognosis?

The hierarchy of formula, as with language, begins with the collection of the smallest sub units of meaning that builds into larger units of meaning. In language, letters are assembled so that they form words, words gathered that form sentences, sentences amassed so that they form paragraphs and so on. The smallest sub unit of formula fiction is the motif. It is the written symbol of an object that functions as a catalyst of a story. It assists in the development of the story's plot and it presents a recognizable cognitive "handle" of the language required by the reader to interpret how a story should be read. To be effective, the motif should suggest a complex of meaning and information that transcends the physical object itself. For example, in traditional Western formula fiction, the motif of the white hat (a symbol of a piece of clothing customarily employed as protection for the head against the sun and rain) assumes moral qualities. It means that its wearer is a "good guy" in the story. Conversely, the owner of the black hat is a "bad guy." The six-shooter can be used to suggest power and virility. The hero's horse can symbolize mobility, while the frontier town can represent civilization and prosperity.

The collection of motifs that takes the basic "words" of the motif and aggregates them into a related group is a motif complex. The motif complex provides the framework of the basic conflict of a section or portion of the story, and it allows linear movement of the story's plot. Employing our Western formula example, a motif complex might be the noon showdown between the good guy and the bad guy, or a chase scene where the hero is hunted by a group of savage Indians. The motif complex is the smallest unit of action in a story, and might correctly be termed "symbols in motion."

The sequence of related motif complex "sentences" that contour a "chapter" of the larger story formula is the sub-formula. The sub-formula stands as the primary basis of the story itself, consisting of a beginning, middle and end of a plot, and it is the smallest unit of a story that effectively resolves the action of the plot. In the traditional Western formula, a number of sub-formulas can be identified, including the railroad story, the ranch empire story, the gunfighter-as-hero story, and so on.

Formula, the next level up on our literary hierarchy, can simply be defined as a collection of thematically connected sub-formulas. It is the "book" of sub-formula "chapters." It provides the largest sub division of story forms and illustrates the boundaries (though certainly flexible and changing) where one grouping of sub-formulas begin and where another ends. Thus, stories that are set in a western, historic American landscape and which submit the hero, villain and other characters of the plot to a series of restricted actions (restricted by the construction of motif complexes and sub-formulas) establish the traditional Western formula.

The largest general unit of a collection of formulas is the genre. It is the "encyclopedia" of a group of formula "books." In American mass-mediated popular print fiction, there are three: the fantasy genre, the mystery genre and the romantic-adventure genre. And these three archetypal story units, collectively deal with the most basic and substantial questions of human existence. The traditional Western formula, assembled with the historical romance, the historic war formula, the contemporary war formula and the sex-money-power formula, would then constitute the romantic-adventure genre.

The literary hierarchy of popular formulas is thus best represented by the pyramid, that most solid of structures, and illustrated would look something like this

GENRE

FORMULA   FORMULA

SUB-FORMULA   SUB-FORMULA   SUB-FORMULA

MOTIF-COMPLEX MOTIF-COMPLEX MOTIF-COMPLEX MOTIF-COMPLEX

MOTIF MOTIF MOTIF MOTIF MOTIF MOTIF MOTIF MOTIF MOTIF

The mystery genre of popular fiction gives us the form of our paper tiger, and since this genre (and its respective formulas, sub-formulas and motifs) is shaded by conflict (between life and death at the most basic level), its creation and its consumption ultimately reflect an attempt on the part of its producers and its audience to rationalize on the nature of death and dying and celebrate the rational (resulting in collective and individual reflection on the systematic and orderly protection of life). With that dichotomy in mind, let us count the stripes of our tiger.

The mystery genre is comprised of six formulas: 1) the supernatural formula, or stories which put man against those forces of the universe which are beyond his understanding or control; 2) the fiction (roman) noir formula, which contain tales of urban pathos and revenge; 3) the gangster formula, or stories of good and bad organized criminals; 4) the thief formula, or those tales of good and bad individual criminals; 5) the thriller, which encompass political suspense stories; and 6) the detective formula, which include stories of the classical, police, hard-boiled and avenger detective heroes.

The paper tiger, snarling creature that he is, has been caught, and now needs to be humanely dissected on our cultural operating table. Let us begin with the mystery genre.

Notes

[1] R.W.B. Lewis, *The American Adam: Innocence, Tragedy and Tradition in the Nineteenth Century* (Chicago: University of Chicago Press, 1955), p. 1.

[2] Frederick Jackson Turner, *The Significance of the Frontier in American History* (New York: Ungar, 1963), p. 27.

[3] Henry Nash Smith, *Virgin Land: The American West as Symbol and Myth* (Cambridge: Harvard University Press, 1950), p. xi.

[4] Richard Slotkin, *Regeneration Through Violence: The Mythology of the American Frontier, 1600-1860* (Middletown: Wesleyan University Press, 1973), p. 8.

[5] *Ibid.*, pp. 6-7.

[6] Peter L. Berger and Thomas Luckmann, *The Social Construction of Reality* (Garden City: Doubleday, 1966), p. 3.

[7] *Ibid.*, p. 4.

[8] Peter L. Berger, *The Sacred Canopy: Elements of a Sociological Theory of Religion* (Garden City: Doubleday, 1967), p. 3.

[9] *Ibid.*, p. 4.

[10] *Ibid.*, p. 13.

[11] *Ibid.*, p. 15.

[12] Berger and Luckmann, pp. 101-102.

[13] John G. Cawelti, *Adventure, Mystery, and Romance* (Chicago: University of Chicago Press, 1976), p. 8.

[14] *Ibid.*, pp. 8-9.

[15] *Ibid.*, p. 9.

[16] *Ibid.*, pp. 11-12.

[17] *Ibid.*, p. 15.

[18] *Ibid.*, pp. 15-16.

[19] *Ibid.*, p. 20.

[20] *Ibid.*, p. 27.

[21]*Ibid.*, pp. 35-36.

[22]Berger, p. 3.

[23]Claude Levi-Strauss, *Structural Anthropology* (New York: Basic Books, 1963), p. 31.

[24]Frank Smith, *Understanding Reading: A Psycholinguistic Analysis of Reading and Learning to Read* (New York: Holt, Rinehart & Winston, 1978), pp. 1-10.

[25]*Ibid.*, p. 2.

[26]*Ibid.*, pp. 7-10.

[27]*Ibid.*, pp. 163-64.

[28]*Ibid.*, p. 169.

CHAPTER II
Mystery Genre

Looking at the Mystery of the Mystery

PEOPLE LOVE TO TALK ABOUT MYSTERY fiction, almost as much as they like to read it. Through the years, a great number of critical works have appeared, written by fans, academics and mystery writers themselves, attempting to analyze in some depth the popularity of one of the most popular types of fiction. Perhaps these critics feel compelled to legitimize in their own minds and to those around them why they respond to stories that deal with murder, violence and the dark inner workings of the human mind. Perhaps they feel a bit guilty in being entertained by fiction that with most writers, at least, makes no pretensions about being a high art, and so they apply the devices of literary criticism to the mystery, implying (or overtly stating), then, that the mystery is of "high" enough quality to be classified as literature. Perhaps there is some more complex reason that can explain the critic's forensic dissection of the body of the popular mystery. The product, however, of all of this attention and classification and rhetorical examination is a muddy soup of terms that, when digested as a whole, leaves one confused about just what dinner was, as can be seen in the following brief survey of several examples of mystery criticism.

Howard Haycraft, for instance, in his book *Murder for Pleasure: The Life and Times of the Detective Story* selectively excludes "mystery stories, crime stories, spy stories [and] even Secret Service stories [that do not] show some authentic detective strain"[1] from the domain of the mystery, concentrating on a single twig of an otherwise massive branch of popular fiction. Haycraft perceives the detective story as a game, with a set of rules for writer and reader participation. He proposes two main requirements for playing the game: "1) The detective story must play fair, (and) 2) The detective story must be readable."[2] Haycraft means by playing fair "that no evidence shall be made known to the reader which remains unknown to the detective; that false clues are automatically forbidden; that fortuity and coincidence are outlawed as beneath the dignity of the self-respecting craftsman; that all determinative action must proceed directly and causatively from the central theme of the crime-and-pursuit; and that no extraneous factors shall be allowed to divert or prolong the plot in any essential manner."[3] For the detective story to be readable, Haycraft states: "that the detective story must avoid becoming a static and immobile puzzle, on the one hand, and that it must forswear the meretricious aid of hokum, on the other."[4] There are two major problems with Haycraft's analysis. First, he divorces the detective story from a meaningful application to the culture and society in which it appears, sterilizing it and ultimately killing it. Haycraft's detective "game" is played by people, not by rhetorical abstracts. And one can always learn more by observing how people play the game than by commenting on the "ideal" structure of the game itself. Second, and more importantly, Haycraft advances the worst sort of self-serving egoism with his rules of the detective story. He is more interested in prescribing what the fiction *should* be than in *describing* what it really is. According to Haycraft, if a particular story does not meet his rules of the game, like Christie's *The Murder of Roger Ackroyd*, it is not a "good" story. The result of this reasoning becomes little more than a guideline of what the critic likes, a statement of personal expectations that may or may not illustrate the reader's expectations.

Linda Herman and Beth Stiel, in their study *Corpus Delicti of Mystery Fiction: A Guide to the Body of the Case*, begin to address the issue of the function of mystery fiction by stating:

There are many basic human needs which the reading of mystery fiction can satisfy. Entertainment, a fine mirroring of the contemporary social scene with its social comment, psychological insight, a modern handling of the Greek idea of catharsis, as well as the mental effort of solving puzzles—these are all there; almost something for everyone.[5]

Herman and Stiel seem to have the "feel" that something sociological is happening in the mystery, but they simply don't possess the critical methodology to examine fully the social aspects of the genre. Their application of the "Greek idea of catharsis" to the mystery can also be easily used with science fiction, romance fiction or fantasy, which, of course, tells us little about the distinctive literary qualities of the mystery itself. Also, the term "catharsis" is more of a topical philosophical notion, with no demonstrable relevance to social function, than a sociological one.

In Nadya Aisenberg's *A Common Spring: Crime Novel and Classic*, the connection between crime fiction and myth is advanced:

Human fears are covertly expressed in the detective story. Detective fiction is inseparable from certain myth making faculties, particularly the imposition of order, through narrative formulae, upon collective fears and uncertainties, and the prevention of rational explanation for inexplicable phenomena.[6]

Aisenberg goes on to say that there is a link between the detective story and other imaginative constructions of the past, such as myth, fairy tale and fable, which thus makes it a natural vehicle for expressing and coping with the moral ambiguities of the present.[7] She also suggests that crime fiction discloses larger truths about the society for which it was written and it can be seen as a way to work out the human conflicts and fears which provide its daily nourishment.[8] Essentially, Aisenberg is correct in the observation of the relationship between myth and mystery fiction, but fails to define what the exact social function of myth is, or how the mystery, as a social device of myth-making, achieves the levels of reality construction that is claimed. Aisenberg's argument is only half-complete, flesh without a skeleton to support it.

H.R.F. Keating, in the introduction to his collection of essays about mystery fiction, *Whodunit? A Guide to Crime, Suspense and Spy Fiction*, presents his perspective, as a successful mystery writer, of what crime fiction really is. He recognizes the attraction of this type of writing for its audience, stating: "The many-headed hybrid [mystery fiction], as I see it, can be said roughly to be fiction that is written primarily as entertainment and has as its subject some form of crime, crime taken in its widest possible meaning."[9] Keating further elaborates on the "entertainment" value of the formula by saying: 1) that the mystery writer sets out simply to hold the reader's attention, and then later, perhaps, to tell him something of social value; 2) that the mystery writer reinforces the legal sanctions of society by showing that "crime does not pay;" 3) that the mystery enters into a kind of "invisible" contract with the reader, promising to entertain him; and 4) that this contract should contain a "flaw" that acts as a concession to the mere need to delight in what is being read.[10] It should indeed be emphasized that the mystery, first and foremost, is a literature of entertainment. No person or power holds a "loaded revolver" to the temple of the prospective reader, forcing him to plunk down cash for the latest John D. MacDonald Travis McGee novel, forcing him to lie in a favorite easy chair or bed to read the new Bill Pronzini anthology of "Nameless Detective" short stories, or forcing him to renew a yearly subscription to the *Ellery Queen's Mystery Magazine*. But the realm of entertainment should be fully defined, which Keating and many other critics do not do. What makes a mystery entertaining? What energy does it have to perpetuate itself in the bookstores and newsstands? By entertainment, does Keating mean education and socialization? These elements demand to be better understood before the critic can comment on the mystery's entertainment value.

These are things that the fans have to say about the mystery. But what does the academic perceive? E.T. Guymon, Jr., in his short essay "Why Do We Read This Stuff?" prepared for inclusion in a mystery course textbook entitled *The Mystery Story* claims:

Mystery fiction is the greatest escape literature of all time. Escape from what? Why, from the reality of problems. We are all armchair detectives and from the safety of that armchair we can identify ourselves with the characters in the book and enjoy the crime, the mystery, the danger, the chase and, very important, the puzzle, the matching of wits and the solution. If interest in the mystery story has increased...it must be because problems—personal, domestic, and foreign— have also increased. In other words, today we have more from which to escape.[11]

Without debating the rather questionable statements that mystery fiction is the "greatest" escape literature (what about fantasy or science fiction for example?) or that we are all "armchair detectives" (I imagine there are those individuals who do not favor this type of detective story), Guymon's contention that the mystery is escapist demonstrates a misuse of the term. The escapist value here does not mean escape *from* the problems of day to day living, but escape *into* those problems (in a pleasant way). The mystery allows the reader to examine social issues better, like murder and theft, by telling stories about their impact upon the lives of fictional characters. If there is a soothing effect upon the reader in reading mystery fiction, it is not because it is a road away from his problems. Instead, by detailing the action and consequences of socially prohibited areas of human life, the mystery assists the reader in better coping with the environment of crime by encouraging a specific scrutiny of crime.

Certainly, one of the most ambitious projects in the academic sphere at developing a formulaic theory describing the social function of the mystery story is John G. Cawelti's *Adventure, Mystery, and Romance*. Unfortunately, however, Cawelti is merely content to rehash those issues (and their respective problems) that have already been covered. For example, Cawelti defines the Mystery as:

... the investigation and discovery of hidden secrets, the discovery usually leading to some benefit for the character(s) with whom the reader identifies. ...In mystery formulas, the problem always has a desirable and rational solution, for this is the underlying moral fantasy expressed in this formulaic archetype.[12]

Cawelti reiterates the contention that the mystery "is primarily an intellectual, reasoning activity" (though he acknowledges that this may entail an expression of nonintellectual or unconscious interests).[13] And he states that the mystery "involves the isolation of clues, the making of deductions from these clues, and the attempt to place the various clues in their rational place in a complete scheme of cause and effect."[14]

Cawelti demonstrates Haycraft's erroneous tendency to mix the formulas of the classical detective story, where there exist the motif complexes of clue isolation and rational deductions, with the balance of mystery genre formulas. Cawelti also implies Herman and Stiel's use of catharsis in the mystery by advocating its rational emotional appeal without describing the underlying sociological justification of that appeal. Finally, Cawelti undermines the power of his argument by stating: "Because of the basic intellectual demands it makes on its audience, the pure mystery has become one of the most sophisticated and explicitly artful of formulaic types."[15] One of the justifications of Cawelti's examination of popular formulas, employing the myth/symbol approach to literature, is to divorce formula fiction from negative "artistic" evaluation, that is, to get away from saying that Poe is inferior to Joyce or that Hammett's *Maltese Falcon* is inferior to James' *The Turn of the Screw*. The question of artistic value does not blend well with the theory of social function, since the former relies much too heavily upon individual taste and less on mass audience function.

This mystery should be examined in four ways. First, a social definition of the mystery genre should be outlined that distinguishes the literary boundaries of the genre from those of other popular genres. Second, a theory should be proposed that describes the educational and socializing functions of the mystery. Third, the myth-making aspect of the mystery should be advanced that emphasizes the process of reality construction. And finally the various sub-formulas of the mystery genre should be clarified so that a confusion of terms can be avoided. Employing the above four-part recipe, let us hunt the beast.

Defining the Mystery Genre

The mystery genre, as one of the three major popular fiction genres that also include fantasy and romantic-adventure, offers a literary spectrum that connects, at opposing ends, the Rational and the Irrational. This literary spectrum mediates the question of the human death crisis. Death is an inevitable fact of existence, which makes people aware of time and their mortality. The Rational end of the mystery genre spectrum provides a socially optimistic explanation of human existence. This end includes those mystery stories which narrate the defeat of evil, the affirmation of good, and which suggest that a positive future for ensuing generations will be guaranteed. The Irrational end of the mystery genre spectum, on the other hand, is basically pessimistic, containing those mystery stories that conversely narrate the triumph of evil over good, and that betoken the individual's precarious position in the universe, buffeted by the winds of a hostile chaos and threatened by destruction (more specifically, death).

The mystery genre can be explained as those collections of formulas and sub-formulas that linearly traverse moral explorations of the human death crisis and that either: 1) uphold death's control of individual and group action, or 2) provide a religious or secular explanation of death that celebrates the power of life. The formulas and sub-formulas of the mystery genre chart the human death crisis in several ways. First, those mystery stories that locate themselves at the Rational end of the linear spectrum present formulaic crisis situations (such as the threat of evil, or more specifically, death) in which secular or religious rituals reinforce the individual's sense of reality. The motif complexes of these stories (the solution of the crime "puzzle" in classical detective fiction, for example) thus become vehicles of the rational. Second, those mystery stories that locate themselves at the Irrational end of the spectrum offer formulaic crisis situations in which meaning and understanding of the universe are denied by others (divine forces or human forces, depending on the sub-formula). And finally, the mystery genre illustrates, either successfully or unsuccessfully, the defeat of man's baser, animal instincts through socialization.[16] It spans the bridge between life and death, between the animal world (the violent, the chaotic, the irrational) and the social world (the secure, the predictable, the rational). It relates stories that define the effectiveness of human action, specifically of the individual's ultimate control and/or understanding of the death crisis.

The mystery genre, collectively, is entertaining because it provides readers with rituals of socialization that reinforce institutions (thus diminishing alienation). This process is called world maintenance. One particular of the function of world maintenance in the mystery genre serves to establish and protect the individual's notion of reality. The mystery story raises the issue of social construction that format evil and good in contextual situations by answering in the story questions about life and death. Mystery fiction, as world maintenance, presents tales that define the frontier of taboo, of institutional control of that frontier, and of the cosmic/human consequences of going past that frontier.[17]

As a literary vehicle for the social construction of reality, the mystery genre is a social device for myth making. The definition of myth in social-psychology serves to explain the mystery's role as myth maker. Myth can be defined as the individual's perception of the sacred intruding upon the world of the profane. Myth making is part of world maintenance, and as such develops collective notions of that relationship between the seen and unseen, the sacred and the profane, cosmic order and human order.[18]

The mythgenesis factor of the mystery genre operates at several levels. Mythology is the most naive tool used in man's understanding of reality.[19] The mystery genre, then, provides a matrix where inconsistent mythological perceptions can co-exist. Thus, the sub-formula of dark fantasy fiction, though seeming to bear little resemblance to the sub-formula of classical detective fiction, is contained in the same larger structure of the mystery genre, since both sub-formulas at the macro-level define the conflict between good and evil, between life-maintenance and death-crisis, though the one convention says: "the Devil made me do it," and the other says: "greed made me do it."

The mystery genre, at another level of the sphere of mythmaking, allows the reader to become expert with his culture. By learning what is accepted, by eliminating what is not consistent with the social norm, the individual reading detective fiction gains knowledge of how to behave in society (by not stealing from one's neighbor or by not killing one's neighbor for his wife), and visualizes the social consequences for unacceptable action (the detective hero places the crook in jail for theft or murder). The individual, by reading supernatural fiction, gains knowledge of God's (or "good") will and witnesses the destructive power of the Devil over those who deviate from God's will. Via mythgenesis, a person's identity is formed, and via the mystery genre, as a spectrum of formulaic interpretations of human action, that identity is educated.

Before we proceed to a more detailed examination of the formulas and sub-formulas of the mystery genre, several points need to be made about the following taxonomy and about the "biological" nature of formula. Formula is like a living creature, a living paper tiger if you will. The definitions of the supernatural formula, or thief formula or detective formula are not static, not set in concrete. They flex and flow and merge with the boundaries of each other. For example, though supernatural fiction and detective fiction exist at opposing poles on the mystery spectrum, one can find stories which feature the ghost-detective hero and that effectively combine elements of both formulas. This can be explained, in part, by the "building block" function of motif complexes. Authors arrange the various blocks of motif complexes to build a sub-formula story. Since popular fiction is a commercial commodity (it is written to be sold for a profit) the author of popular fiction strives to build a story that both meets the larger cultural expectations of entertainment and the specific needs of the audience. The story that relies too much on the former becomes static, or boring, and the story that exclusively courts the latter becomes topical, and boring, because of its tendency for being so quickly "outdated." The result of this process is a "survival of the fittest" popular fiction. If an arrangement of motif complexes demonstrates financial success at the bookstore, then it is imitated until it stops selling. If that same arrangement is commercially unsuccessful, then it dies. Formula fiction seeks new combinations of survival, and so evolves, but not too fast nor too slow. The following taxonomy offers axial touchstones of the mystery genre that serve to locate the generalized centers of the formula types since it is virtually impossible to delineate their definite boundaries.

The formula of the mystery genre that lies closest to the Irrational end of the linear spectrum is the supernatural story. The supernatural formula includes those stories which investigate the relationship between life and death, and which assume the form of a conflict between human being and nature (or supernature), with the human being recognizing that the power of nature is far greater. The protagonist, or hero, of this formula during the course of the conflict is diminished in stature, or destroyed, and death, as agent of nature, is perceived as, at best, incomprehensible, and, at worst, dominant. Rational explanations of the individual's place in his universe are subservient to the irrational; evil is more powerful than good; the Devil more prominent than God. The dark fantasy sub-formula contains fiction where nature is totally evil and ruled by the Devil. Any conflict between the individual and nature *always* results in the individual's destruction. Knowledge itself becomes evil, and is of little use against the agents of nature

This sub-formula represents the most pessimistic vision of the individual's relationship with the unknown. In the Gothic sub-formula, nature assumes the role of Fate and is a hostile power against the individual. Natural disasters, represented as earthquakes or storms, assume the dimensions of divine will, and the individual possesses little chance for survival unless he complies with this divine will. The traditional supernatural variant produces a story where the supernatural assumes an anthropomorphic form (like a ghost, vampire or werewolf) and this "monster" further demonstrates the superior force in its conflict with the individual. To battle the "children of the night" (symbolic of the individual's dread of the unknown and unseeable) the protagonist needs special religious icons of power. Though the individual may "put to rest" the monster, it is understood that the power of evil survives and ultimately cannot be destroyed. In the psycho-killer sub-formula, supernatural motif complexes are less evident. Here, socially deviant antagonists prey on their fellows, and the basic makeup of the individual's moral fiber is defined as being evil. The protagonist, usually female, undergoes an ordeal of violence in an attempt (mostly unsuccessful) to survive death.

Next closest to the Irrational end is the fiction noir formula, and as with the supernatural formula, the conflict between human beings and nature is featured, but with a variation. Nature is represented as Fate (but not of supernatural dimension), and Fate is symbolized by urban society itself (government, police, the law). The individual is "trapped" by his own evil actions and suffers at the hands of an even more evil social system. The light-angel sub-formula highlights an avenging figure protagonist who strives to liberate an innocent victim from the "jaws" of misdirected justice, while the dark-angel sub-formula also highlights an avenging figure who directs the forces of Fate against the innocent (and guilty) victims of social persecution.

Next, the gangster formula features a collection of deviants who strive to rebel against the larger social order, employing unlawful means to gather more and more power within the social structure, and symbolizing a microcosm of evil within the macrocosm of evil society. The good gangster sub-formula portrays this collection of deviants as protagonists who desire a higher form of justice, opposing those who manipulate the law for evil purposes, while the bad gangster sub-formula portrays the collection of deviants as antagonists who desire to manipulate the law and social order to their advantage.

Closer to the Rational end of the mystery genre linear spectrum is the thief formula, which has the protagonist as an "outcast," or rebel, of society. The thief endeavors to break the laws of society to further the cause of his own monetary gain. As in the gangster sub-formula, society is viewed as being corrupt and deserving of "rape." The good thief sub-formula, though the protagonist is a rebel figure, transgresses social law to achieve a type of justice which is above the corrupt standards of society, and the bad thief sub-formula presents the thief as a villain who steals the icons of society (i.e., money, jewels) to further his own financial gain.

The thriller formula, next on the spectrum, characterizes those stories which are political adventures and which illustrate nationalistic ideologies in conflict. The respective agents of adversary governments battle each other in order to insure the continuation of their worldview on a global level. The charismatic spy sub-formula features a hero who operates in a world where the definitions of "right" and "wrong" are clearly defined. The charismatic spy, often representing Western governments (i.e. the United States or Great Britain) employs physical strength, courage and guile in defeating hostile agents (of the Communist countries). The dark spy sub-formula presents a more complex and morally ambiguous view of world politics, where the definitions of right and wrong are less clearly defined. The dark spy recognizes the fallacy of his country's ideology, yet still pursues the successful completion of his assigned task, despite doubts.

At the Rational end of the mystery genre spectrum is, finally, the detective formula. Here the mystery of life and death is fully symbolized as a puzzle, which possesses a solution. The detective hero is the puzzle-solver who attempts (and succeeds) to dispense rational explanations of irrational events (i.e., murder and theft). The individual, as detective hero, is in total control of Fate, justice and even death itself. Though evil exists, it can be controlled, and even be destroyed by the hero. In the classical detective sub-formula, crime is seen as a puzzle which can *always* be solved given the right set of clues and the right puzzle-solver. The classical detective hero is an eccentric, leisure class protagonist who maintains the benevolent social order and who protects those symbols of the leisure class (i.e. money, jewels) from working class thieves. The police detective sub-formula features a hero who, unlike his amateur classical counterpart, is a bureaucratic professional (the policeman) but who, like the classical detective hero, also protects the "standards" of society from the criminal classes. The hard-boiled detective sub-formula highlights an individual who recognizes the positive qualities of law and justice, even if those positive qualities are clouded by layers of social corruption. Often working against the system he is defending, the hard-boiled detective hero strives for his own personal code of honor, his own personal satisfaction in a job "well done," rather than for fame or wealth and lastly, the avenger-detective sub-formula presents a vigilante hero who by-passes the social processes of law, acting as judge, jury and executioner in his quest to rid society of evil that society itself cannot handle.

The following chapters, which select and feature the short story or novel that originated (or best represents) a particular mystery genre sub-formula (while placing that work in a historical and cultural context), will follow the Irrational/Rational linear spectrum as it progresses from one end to the other, and each specific chapter will track the historical literary evolution of the various mystery sub-formulas as they developed in popular mass-mediated print formula entertainment.

Notes

[1]Howard Haycraft, *Murder for Pleasure: The Life and Times of the Detective Story* (New York: Carroll & Graf Publishers, 1984), p. x.

[2]*Ibid.*, p. 225.

[3]*Ibid.*, p. 226.

[4]*Ibid.*

[5]Linda Herman and Beth Stiel, *Corpus Delicti of Mystery Fiction: A Guide to the Body of the Case* (Metuchen: Scarecrow Press, 1974), p. 1.

[6]Nadya Aisenberg, *A Common Spring: Crime Novel & Classic* (Bowling Green: Bowling Green University Popular Press, 1979), p. 1.

[7]*Ibid*, p. 2.

[8]*Ibid.*

[9]H.R.F. Keating, *Whodunit? A Guide to Crime, Suspense and Spy Fiction* (New York: Van Nostrand, Reinhold, 1982), p. 7.

[10]*Ibid.*, pp. 8-9.

[11]E.T. Guymon, Jr., "Why Do We Read This Stuff?" *The Mystery Story*, ed. John Ball, (Del Mar, CA.: Univ. of California, San Diego, 1976), p. 362.

[12]John G. Cawelti, *Adventure, Mystery, and Romance* (Chicago: Univiversity of Chicago Press, 1976), pp. 42-43.

[13]*Ibid.*, p. 43.

[14]*Ibid.*

[15]*Ibid.*

[16]Peter L. Berger and Thomas Luckmann, *The Social Construction of Reality* (Garden City: Doubleday, 1966), p. 180.

[17]Peter L. Berger, *The Sacred Canopy: Elements of a Sociological Theory of Religion* (Garden City: Doubleday and Company, 1967), p. 48.

[18]Berger and Luckmann, p. 110.

[19]*Ibid.*

CHAPTER III
Supernatural Formula

The Gothic Foundation

IT SEEMS SOMEHOW FITTING FOR a literary formula wrapped in the shroud of the supernatural to have been invented in a dream, if one can believe Horace Walpole's statement written in a letter dated March 9, 1765. Discussing the inspiration leading to the writing of his short novel *The Castle of Otranto* (1764), Walpole states: "I thought myself in an ancient castle (a very natural dream for a head filled like mine with Gothic story) and that on the uppermost banister of a great staircase I saw a gigantic hand in armour. In the evening I sat down and began to write, without knowing in the very least what I intended to say or relate."[1] Walpole's disclosure, whether concocted for the amusement of his friends (as writers tend to do from time to time, fanning their ego and deliberately mystifying the rather mundane process of setting words on paper) or actual truth, establishes a tripod of motif complexes that shore-up the foundation of the Gothic sub-formula: the Gothic building (or castle), the aberration of nature and the dream.

Horace Walpole (1717-1797), in addition to being a member of the English Parliament for the Borough of Callington, Cornwall, a poet and author of some thirty-eight books and an art critic of meager reputation, was a self-styled apostle of romanticism and an antiquarian. His particular interests merged with his fascination for Gothic architecture, and being able to indulge his avocation in the most theatrical way, using his abundant income bequeathed to him on his father's death in 1745, he purchased and remodeled his own miniature "Gothic castle" at Strawberry Hill near Twickenham in 1749.

As an antiquarian scholar, Walpole was aware of the dual nature of the Gothic tradition. On the one hand, the term "Gothic" suggested to the Renaissance mind gloomy castles, dark and barbaric structures erected in savage, unenlightened times. And yet, by the middle of the eighteenth century, with the emergence of the democratic-romantic side of the Renaissance, Gothic came to be identified by the antiquarians with imagination, vastness and mystery.[2] Walpole facilitated the transition of the Gothic ideal into literature with *The Castle of Otranto*, which became quite popular with an emerging middle class English readership and which subsequently dominated the form and formula of popular fiction for the next one hundred years.

The overriding symbol directing the plot structure of *The Castle of Otranto* is the castle itself (from which the novel derives its title), the first leg of the Gothic tripod, and Walpole employs this symbol in several significant ways. First, the environs of the castle and the principality of Otranto serve as an emblem of political power. Manfred, the usurping Prince of Otranto and principal villain of the story, seeks to solidify his hold on the kingdom by circumventing an ancient prophecy, which states: "That the castle and lordship of Otranto should pass from the present family, whenever the real owner should be grown too large to inhabit it."[3] This prophecy assumes the dimension of a divine curse over the course of the story as Manfred is thwarted in his Machiavellian attempts to consolidate his rule and perpetuate his political lineage. The prophecy, also, ironically, doubles as a supernatural pun as the reader discovers later on. By demonstrating the ability of heaven to intercede in Manfred's schemings, and indeed to control the very actions of the story's characters through supernatural agents, Walpole is suggesting that human action is ruled by forces beyond human control. Second, the castle becomes a stage for the movements of the characters. Besides the wicked Manfred, the cast—including Hippolita, Manfred's faithful wife, Matilda, his doomed daughter, Isabella, the object of Manfred's immoral desires, Theodore, the protagonist of the story and human adversary of Manfred, and Father Jerome, disclosed "father of Theodore" and officer of the church—play an elaborate game of hide-and-seek with one another through the dark shadows and hidden corridors of the castle. Behind the next locked door is salvation, or a monster:

"My lord," said Jaquez, "when Diego and I came into the gallery, he went first, for he said he had more courage than I. So when we came into the gallery, we found nobody .... When we came to the door of the great chamber," continued Jaquez, "we found it shut .... I! my lord!" said Jaquez, "I saw nothing; I was behind Diego;—but I heard the noise .... Diego had no sooner opened the door, then he cried out and ran back—I ran back too, and said 'Is it the ghost? The ghost!' 'No, no,' said Diego, and his hair stood on end—'it is a giant, I believe; he is clad in armour, for I saw his foot and part of his leg'...."[4]

Down the passage is freedom, or entrapment:

The lower part of the castle was hollowed into several intricate cloisters; and it was not easy for one under so much anxiety to find the door that opened into the cavern. An awful silence reigned throughout those subterraneous regions, except now and then some blasts of wind that shook the doors she [Isabella] had passed, and which grating on the rusty hinges were reechoed through that long labyrinth of darkness. Every murmur struck her with new terror . . . .[5]

The process of revelation, of uncovering the layers of deception to get at the truth, which on one level is the quest to discover the lawful ruler of Otranto and on another is the quest to discover the will of God, is mirrored by the castle. The funhouse, trapdoor, revolving wall, spook-around-the-corner special effect qualities of the castle formulaically demonstrate the seeming impossibility of understanding truth. The castle can never be fully understood, only lived in; the will of God can never be known, only obeyed. Open the wrong door and the ghost gets you. Defy heaven and God gets you. Finally then, the castle, Walpole implies, is a state-of-mind, an atmosphere, and this state-of-mind bequeaths a promise and an affliction. The promise is that evil acts, as perpetuated by Manfred, will be punished. For all his conspiracies, Manfred's children and ambition are destroyed: his son, Conrad, crushed beneath a gigantic helmet that magically falls from the sky at the outset of the story; his daughter, Matilda, accidentally slain by his own hand at the conclusion of the story; his leadership overthrown by the rightful ruler, Theodore and his self-imposed banishment (along with his wife's) to a neighboring convent secured. The affliction is that even though "good will conquer evil," as orchestrated by heaven, the resulting trauma of the conflict produces unhappiness. Though Theodore acquires the principality of Otranto and the offer of marriage of the (still) chaste Isabella, the loss of Matilda, his true love, condemns him to a future where "he could know no happiness," and where melancholy takes possession of his soul.

The castle, as dominating symbol of the Gothic sub-formula, offers a specific example of a symbolic interpretation of a social institution.[6] Symbols can be defined as the cognitive "tagging" of meaningful thoughts, actions and emotions to objects and ideas. The Gothic castle here represents, as a symbol, a world where human thought and human action can be meaningfully placed. The castle of *The Castle of Otranto* reflects a mind-set that defines the importance of good and evil within the larger context of life and death. The dynamics of moral status form the second leg of Walpole's Gothic tripod, that being the motif complex of the aberration of nature.

The Castle of Otranto offers two examples of the aberration of nature: human-inspired and supernatural-inspired, though often the one acts as a catalyst for the other. In the Gothic, the most common manifestation of human-inspired aberration is the violation of sexual mores. After Manfred's designs to marry his son, Conrad, to Isabella (and thus legitimize his rule by cleaving to the "rightful" bloodline of Otranto) are defeated (with the gigantic helmet crushing Conrad before the wedding can be completed), he devises a new course of action and proposes marriage to Isabella himself:

"I desired you once before," said Manfred angrily, "not to name that woman [Hippolita]; from this hour she must be a stranger to you, as she must be to me:—in short, Isabella, since I cannot give you my son, I offer you myself . . . ."[7]

Isabella's reply to Manfred's outrageous offer sums up his sexual transgressions: " 'Heaven!' cried Isabella, waking from her delusion, 'what do I hear! You, my lord! You! My father in law! the father of Conrad! the husband of the virtuous and tender Hippolita![8] Isabella' " quickly escapes the advances of Manfred, escapes into the depths of the castle to secure refuge, with Manfred in lusting pursuit. Manfred's shocking action is socially defined for the reader as shocking because: 1) the marriage violates the relationship between in-laws; 2) Manfred demonstrates disrespect for his dead son and to his "house guest," Isabella; 3) Manfred's desire to divorce his wife, Hippolita, is motivated primarily by political ambition and this is a betrayal of the sanctity of marriage; and 4) the disregard of social custom with his advances insults the traditional ideal of male-female chivalry. Manfred's sexual misconduct assumes the dimensions of an aberration of nature since his actions challenge the social roles and institutions (like marriage) that are maintained by powerful religious legitimations. And since institutions formed from social definitions of human sexuality are connected to a sacred thread, the violation of the sacred becomes the violation of "natural law."[9] *The Castle of Otranto*, then, narrates the supernatural intervention that frustrates Manfred's aberrant sexual behavior and consequently outlines the boundaries of taboo (formulaically). Manfred is unable to consummate his lust for Isabella, which would also represent a consummation of his lust for political power, since she eludes his clutches and is hidden in the depths of the castle itself (hidden by God's will), ironically, the very object of his self-serving ambition. As Manfred pursues Isabella, he is warned by supernatural encroachments into the mortal world to cease and desist, which he rationalizes away or ignores (further incurring the wrath of heaven), and at the story's conclusion is punished for his violations of natural law. The primary conflicts of the Gothic sub-formula are between the individual and heaven, free will and fate, human action and supernatural retribution. Walpole places Manfred at the one end of this conflict, and arms him with his craftiness and guile. At the other end assembled against Manfred are the forces of heaven, representing themselves as supernatural powers. Manfred acts, and supernature reacts. His maneuver to marry his son to Isabella is checked by the supernatural death of Conrad. His rape of Isabella is countered by supernatural manifestations of gigantic armor (belonging to the specter, Alfonso the Good) magically appearing throughout the castle, which frighten his servants and impede their search. His schemes to cheat the ancestors of Alfonso of their divine right to rule Otranto are befuddled by supernatural gusts of wind and claps of thunder. And finally, the demands of heaven bring the very walls of the castle to the ground:

A clap of thunder at that instant shook the castle to its foundations; the earth rocked, and the clank of more than mortal armour was heard. Frederic and Jerome thought the last day was at hand. The latter, forcing Theodore along with them, rushed into the court. The moment Theodore appeared, the walls of the castle behind Manfred was thrown down by a mighty force, and the form of Alfonso, dilated to an immense magnitude, appeared in the center of the ruins. "Behold in Theodore, the true heir of Alfonso!" said the vision: and having pronounced these words, accompanied by a clap of thunder, it ascended solemnly towards heaven ....[10]

Manfred's human-inspired aberration of natural law is rebuffed by supernatural-inspired aberration. Human free-will is an ineffectual force against divine will. The sociological function of supernaturalism in the Gothic is an interesting social statement, a vehicle of "death-definition," if you will, that shapes the form of religious inquiry, that sparks the quest for the meaning of life. The use of supernaturalism in Gothic fiction functions as a world-maintaining and a world-destroying device: world destroying in that it threatens the individual with an unpleasant outcome of the death crisis dilemma (the ghost will get you if you break nature's law); world-maintaining in that it encourages identification with spiritual good (God, for example). Thus, definitions of good, as embodied by the ghost Alfonso and the human Theodore in *The Castle of Otranto* assumes the dimensions of sacred truth within the formula of the fiction, and the individual holds in his hands a type of cultural "roadmap" which directs him to salvation (eternal life). Mortal destruction, as evidenced by Manfred's downfall, is assured if "good" is denied or dismissed.

The third leg of Walpole's tripod of Gothic motif complexes the dream, is the most revealing in a social-psychological way of the nature of Gothic foundation of the mystery genre. If the various sub-formulas of the mystery genre may be arranged in a sociological spectrum that recounts the certainty of life or the chaos or death, then, the Gothic end of that spectrum defines alienation leading to meaninglessness.

The Gothic tradition, which evolves later, historically, into the supernatural, dark fantasy and psycho-killer sub-formulas, basically charts the instability of human society.[11] The castle, symbol of the Gothic story, is but a further symbol of death. Its foundation is placed on the edge of meaninglessness and it is an edifice that sways from the wind of powerful evil forces of destruction. The Gothic, as a story of death, locates the edge of meaninglessness and illustrates the "road" away from alienation, back from the inevitability of death, back to the institutions of raitionality and life.

The Supernatural Frame

The effect of Walpole's *The Castle of Otranto* upon the literary community of popular fiction was both profound and far-reaching. It wasn't so much that he demonstrated mastery over the sub-formula of the Gothic story: his presentation of the narrative within the restricting confines of the Medieval Romance and his utilization of a cliche-framing device (claiming the story was translated from an antique Italian manuscript discovered "in the library of an ancient catholic family in the north of England") bog down the force of the "episodes" of terror; rather, it was the inspiration that he had on other authors (who more effectively carried his tripod of motif complexes to outrageous limits) that highlighted his contribution to the mystery genre. And for the next several decades, the Gothic held a vice-like grip upon the reins of the popular press in Europe. William Beckford's *Vathek* (1786) featured an even more villainous version of Walpole's Manfred, the Caliph Vathek, who could kill with his evil eye. Ann Radcliffe's *The Mysteries of Udolpho* (1794) placed the vulnerable and sensitive Emily St. Aubert in the perilous castle, Udolpho, while Matthew Lewis' *Ambrosio, or The Monk* (1796) chronicled the seduction of the pious monk, Ambrosio, by a female demon, Matilda, who transforms the erstwhile holy man into a murderer, an incestuous rapist and a Satanic disciple. Mary Shelley's *Frankenstein, or The Modern Prometheus* (1818) narrated the tragic downfall of the scientist, Victor Frankenstein, who attempts in his God-like vanity to create human life, but who ultimately manufactures catastrophe for himself, his friends and his "monster."

Interestingly, the "social get-together" which inspired the young Shelley to write *Frankenstein* also inspired another author, John Polidori (1795-1821), to draft one of the earliest examples in popular fiction of the traditional supernatural sub-formula, "The Vampyre: a Tale" (1819). Polidori was Lord Byron's physician and one of the group of travelers who vacationed at Lake Geneva in June 1816, and, bored with the poor weather, who dared each other to write a ghost story. From this contest, Shelley wrote *Frankenstein*; Percy Shelley, her husband, failed to produce anything of consequence; Byron also failed to complete a story (though he revised the fragment he *did* author then later into a tale called "The Burial" in 1817); and Polidori, borrowing heavily from the popular Gothic novelists of the time, developed the first literary vampire story. Unfortunately, Poldori possessed more ego than writing talent, and after separating from his mentor, Byron, lacked the ability to generate the past success that he had with "The Vampyre," and falling into heavy debt, committed suicide at age 26.

Polidori's "The Vampyre" underwent a number of reprintings, becoming quite popular with the readers of the time. Part of this popularity stemmed from Polidori's synthesis of two shopworn formulaic traditions into a singularly inventive narrative. On one level, Polidori captured certain antiquarian supernatural motifs from oral folktales, something which had not been accomplished before in the development of the mystery genre (such as the particulars of the vampire legend), and he fashioned these motifs into a literate, terrifying articulation of contemporary horror. In other words, Polidori took the vampire out of the cultural backwaters of central and southern Europe and placed him in the elegant parlors of the noble rich, thus transforming an otherwise quaint "country spook" into a more frightening creation, more frightening because Polidori understood what *really* scared his readers.

Certainly "The Vampyre" contained its fair share of Gothic supernatural trappings, as shall be discussed later on, but more importantly, it scratched at that secular nerve of the middle class: economic ruin. Polidori counterposes a naive, innocent orphan named Aubrey against the dark vampire nobleman, Lord Ruthven, and with this moral dichotomy shaped into the forms of the protagonist and antagonist of the story, Polidori describes the relationship between evil and money:

Hitherto, Aubrey had had no opportunity of studying Lord Ruthven's character, and now he found, that, though many more of his actions were exposed to his view, the results offered different conclusions from the apparent motives to his conduct. His companion was profuse in his liberality—the idle, the vagabond, and the beggar, received from his hand more than enough to relieve their immediate wants. But Aubrey could not avoid remarking, that it was not upon the virtuous, reduced to indigence by the misfortunes attendant even upon virtue, that he bestowed his alms—these were sent from the door with hardly suppressed sneers; but when the profligate came to ask something, not to relieve his wants, but to allow him to wallow in his lust, or to sink him still deeper in his iniquity, he was sent away with rich charity.[12]

Lord Ruthven, as supernatural agent of evil, employs the secular bludgeon of greed to manifest evil's power over men:

There was one circumstance about the charity of his Lordship, which was still more impressed upon his mind: all those upon whom it was bestowed, inevitably found that there was a curse upon it, for they were all either led to the scaffold, or sunk to the lowest and the most abject misery. At Brussels, and other towns through which they passed, Aubrey was surprised at the apparent eagerness with which his companion sought for the centres of all fashionable vice; there he entered into all the spirit of the faro table: he betted, and always gambled with success, except when the known sharper was his antagonist, and then he lost even more than he gained; but it was always with the same unchanging face, with which he generally watched society around: it was not, however, so when he encountered the rash youthful novice, or the luckless father of a numerous family; then his very wish seemed fortune's law—this apparent abstractedness of mind was laid aside, and his eyes sparkled with more fire than that of the cat whilst dallying with the half-dead field mouse. In every town, he left the formerly affluent youth, torn from the circle he adorned, cursing, in the solitude of a dungeon, the fate that had drawn him within the reach of this fiend; whilst many a father sat frantic, amidst the speaking looks of mute hungry children, without a single farthing of his late immense wealth, wherewith to buy even sufficient to satisfy their present craving.[13]

Aubrey soon begins to suspect that Lord Ruthven is more than human, that he is "something supernatural." Polidori's identification of the anomic social event of the individual's economic debacle (in the gambling dens, for example) as engineered by malevolent forces of anthropomorphized evil—the vampire—which perverts innocence into depravity, youthful folly into misery, illustrates the origin of this anomic event in the scheme of things. True, the individual is the cause of economic debacle in the gambling dens, but he is motivated by a supernatural power beyond his understanding. Hence, if natural disasters can be explained in nomic terms, so can the misfortunes that people inflict upon one another in the course of their social interaction.

"Why does God permit some people to eat and others to go hungry?"[14]—or more germane to Polidori's story, "Why does God permit human beings to squander their wealth?" The vampire provides an explanation for this question and is an illustration of the economic inequalities in society, a type of "opiate" to justify the seemingly unexplainable issues of status and wealth, and functions as a symbol to prevent class rebellion.[15] Here, the vampire essentially *is* a social explanation of poverty. Polidori tells us that there are creatures out there which not only consume the individual's lifeforce, but his property as well.

On another level, Polidori's literary success with "The Vampyre" resulted from his manipulation of the Gothic tradition, altering the focus of its subject. From Walpole, Polidori utilized the motif complexes of supernatural-inspired and human-inspired aberrations of nature. In the first paragraph of the story, the author clues the reader in on Ruthven's physical *difference*:

[Ruthven] gazed upon the mirth around him, as if he could not participate therein. Apparently, the light laughter of the fair only attracted his attention, that he might by a look quell it, and throw fear into those breasts where thoughtlessness reigned. Those who felt this sensation of awe, could not explain whence it arose: some attributed it to the dead gray eye, which fixing upon the subject's face, did not seem to penetrate, and at one glance to pierce through to the inward workings of the heart; but feel upon the cheek with a leaden ray that weighed upon the skin it could not pass.[16]

Lord Ruthven, as a supernatural-inspired aberration of nature, paradoxically is drawn by gaiety and laughter, but only to bring its destruction. And his vision, which is uninterested in the beauty of the human shell, hungers for the wickedness of the human heart. His vision, in the greater sense of the term, is cast by his dead gray eye, the eye of the dead, and this physical mark (the mark of evil, no doubt) inspires awe among mankind. The most dramatic example of Ruthven's supernatural power, his ability to rise from death, is generally indicative of the sub-formula as a whole. While traveling in Greece, Aubrey and Ruthven are attacked by a band of robbers. Ruthven receives what appears to be his mortal wounds, and while on his death bed, he forces Aubrey to swear an oath: " 'that for a year and a day you [Aubrey] will not impart your knowledge of my crimes or death to any living being in any way, whatever may happen, or whatever you may see.' "[17] Aubrey complies, though later his oath to Ruthven brings about his own and his sister's undoing. Aubrey returns to the spot where he witnessed Ruthven's death to bury him, but discovers instead a miraculous situation:

> Rising early in the morning, he was about to enter the hovel in which he had left the corpse, when a robber met him, and informed him that it was no longer there, having been conveyed by himself and comrades, upon his retiring, to the pinnacle of a neighboring mount, according to the promise they had given his lordship, that it should be exposed to the first cold ray of the moon that rose after his death. Aubrey was astonished, and taking several of the men, determined to go and bury it upon the spot where it lay. But, when he had mounted to the summit he found no trace of either the corpse or the clothes, though the robbers swore they pointed out the identical rock on which they had laid the body.[18]

Polidori employs the above scene as a symbolic, evil perversion of Christ's resurrection—a perversion since Ruthven uses his supernatural gift to destroy people while Christ uses his gift to "save" people. But both Christ's and Ruthven's resurrection sociologically operate in a similar sphere. The attractiveness of the supernatural sub-formula for its audience assumes religious dimensions; hence, the fundamental dilemma of the death crisis is explored. Supernaturalism, specifically the question of the individual's mortality, outlines the course for a collective meaning of death. Knowledge of the individual's lack of control over his life is explored, and an understanding that death cannot be denied and that lost goals will never be attained during life is made obvious. Mortality is the victim of death's hold on life. But the individual possesses strength in numbers, and where the individual is merely mortal, the social group is immortal.[19] The death of the individual may seem meaningless; the group, as a permanent institution, provides continuity and the history of the individual is encased within a larger context, a context that possesses meaning.[20] A place beyond death, as evidence in the Christian faith where membership is granted those who hold the particular belief in an afterlife, suggests that mortal misfortunes may be ultimately overcome by entrance into an immortal "afterlife."

A further example of Polidori's use of a Gothic motif complex is the manner in which the vampire, Ruthven, employs his supernatural power to seduce innocent women. Aubrey's naive and beautiful young female companion, the Greek Ianthe, is the first victim to be sexually and mortally consumed by the vampire. The result of Ruthven's attack is described in sensual terms:

> There was no colour upon her cheek, not even upon her lip; yet there was a stillness about her face that seemed almost as attaching as the life that once dwelt there—upon her neck and breast was blood, and upon her throat were the marks

of teeth having opened the vein....[21]

Ianthe's death represents that relationship between sex and mortality which in the Gothic is a reflection of the human-inspired aberration of nature. It is a cause-effect relationship. Exaggerated sexual lust is destructive and "evil." And if this lust is not kept in check, it will annihilate innocence, leaving nothing more than a corpse with a magnificent "hickey" to ponder upon. Ruthven's killing of Ianthe is a foreshadowing of a greater sexual crime later in the story, but it also provides a singular episode of a common supernatural motif complex: the conflict between the force of knowledge and the force of superstition. After their first meeting in Greece, Ianthe tells Aubrey of her belief of vampires and their horrible deeds. Aubrey refuses to accept Ianthe's belief, even though he himself has witnessed Ruthven's seeming "supernatural" ability to corrupt kindness and innocence, sucking these human qualities and drawing strength from their destruction. Aubrey refuses to accept the knowledge of vampires, and his refusal to wield this force against evil immediately results in Ianthe's death and the foretokened extermination of Aubrey's sister (and himself) by Ruthven.

Polidori sets the stage of Aubrey's sister's destruction by granting Aubrey knowledge of Ruthven's dark nature (via his observation of Ianthe's vampiric murder and Ruthven's magical resurrection). This time, however, Aubrey is unable to do anything with this knowledge since he has vowed to Ruthven his silence. Ruthven courts and marries Aubrey's sister (a supreme token of the Gothic sexual crime) while Aubrey is impotent to act, bound by his honor as a gentleman and tortured by his knowledge of Ruthven. Approaching death, and unable to contact his sister and warn her, Aubrey finally informs his sister's guardians of his terrible knowledge. They rush to protect Miss Aubrey, but arrive too late. Her marriage to Ruthven is "solemnized," her innocence and beauty used to "glut the thirst of a Vampyre!" Polidori's formulaic reversal of the Christian marriage (which evolves from the Gothic aberration motif complex) is a sociological investigation of the function of religious institutions. Following the proper rituals of the religious institutions (the Christian marriage, for example), the gifts obtained will insure divine blessings, the blessings of the parents and of the parents' offspring, thus insuring future social stability. However to consciously or unconsciously defy the power of religious institutions and their rituals (as with Aubrey haplessly allowing his sister to marry a creature of evil!), this promotes chaos and destruction. To deny proper ritual is to adhere to the forces of the Devil, and the Devil symbolizes disorder and moral death.[22]

Polidori's ultimate contribution to the supernatural sub-formula of the mystery genre is his embodiment of evil within the armature of a single character, a supernatural antagonist. In the Gothic, the conflict between human nature and supernature is housed within the confines of the setting, the castle symbol. In the supernatural tale, the individual confronts not the castle (and all its representations) but the creature. The individual recognizes that the power of the creature over life and death (and over his soul) is far greater than his own. The protagonist during the course of the conflict is diminished in stature (either being killed or damned) and destroyed, and death, as contained within the creature, is perceived as, at best, incomprehensible, and, at worst, dominant. Rational explanations of the individual's place in the universe are subservient to the irrational; evil is more powerful than good, the Devil more prominent in the world than God. This type of story, naturally, advocates adherence to the positive side of religious legitimation, since socially, the alternative is horrifying.

Though there are many examples of the supernatural sub-formula in popular fiction, historically, three major types have evolved. The first type, created by Polidori, is the vampire tale, and from his invention has sprung a number of popular treatments. J.M. Rymer's *Varney the Vampire* (1845) was an English "penny dreadful" commercial success, while Bram Stoker's *Dracula* (1897) was to become a sensation not only as a novel, but as stage and screen treatments as well. Today the vampire story enjoys continued success as evidenced in Stephen King's bestseller, *Salem's Lot* (1975). The second major type of supernatural story is the werewolf tale, and from G.W.M. Reynold's penny dreadful, *Wagner, the Wher-Wolf* (1847), to Clemence Housman's "The Werewolf" (1890), to Jack Williamson's *Darker Than You Think* (1940), the werewolf tale (like the vampire tale) has been well-received in print, as well as in other media. Finally, the ghost tale represents the third major type of supernatural story, and perhaps is the most widespread of the three in popular fiction. Motif complexes of the ghost tale have appeared as early as pre-print folklore, and have contributed a role in a number of early and middle English literary works. But the ghost tale itself became popularized in fiction with the collections of J. Sheridan LeFanu, *Ghost Stories and Tales of Mystery* (1851), M.R. James, *Ghost Stories of an Antiquary* (1904) and with Shirley Jackson's novel *The Haunting of Hill House* (1959).

The supernatural tale was so widespread in the burgeoning mass press of Victorian Europe and America that by the turn of the nineteenth century, various elements (like the chain-rattling specter) started to become cliche for its audience. The dark fantasy tale grew as a literary response to this over-conventionalization.

The Dark Fantasy Revolution

Dark fantasy, the next most recent development within the supernatural formula, emerged in America during the 1920s and was the product of several converging cultural and business influences, including World War I and the rise of the pulp magazine entertainment industry. As American business witnessed unparalleled economic expansion during the 1920s, so did the pulp magazines. Though yet to witness the apex of their popularity in the 1930s, the pulps extended their foothold as a print mass medium by increasing their publication runs, decreasing their cover prices and diversifying their subjects. Pulp magazine publishers began expanding and solidifying their market, subsequently discovering (or rediscovering what dime novel publishers had known several decades earlier) the allure of inexpensive, highly formulaic, highly imaginative fiction. Along with specialized detective fiction pulp magazines, including *Black Mask, Detective Fiction Weekly* and *Ten Detective Aces*, specialized Western fiction pulp magazines, including *Street and Smith's Wild West Weekly*, and specialized romance pulp magazines, the supernatural story pulp magazine, *Weird Tales*, (1923) first appeared during this period of pulp magazine expansion and became the single most influential fiction publication of this formula in America for the next thirty years.

The very nature of today's fantasy, science fiction and supernatural paperback and hardcover markets was dramatically affected by the popular literary motif complexes first advanced in the pages of *Weird Tales*. The three most influential authors published by *Weird Tales* included Texan, Robert E. Howard, who originated the so-called "swords and sorcery" story featuring his brawny heroes, King Kull and Conan, California poet Clark Ashton Smith, who published fiction incorporating a bizarre blend of horror fantasy and science fiction set in tongue-twisting locales like Zothique and Hyperboria, and perhaps most importantly, Howard Phillips Lovecraft, whose refinement of the Gothic sub-formula gave birth to dark fantasy.

Lovecraft was not necessarily a prolific fiction writer. He concentrated much of his efforts on a handful of genre pulp magazines, often openly disdaining the "professional" wordsmith. Instead, during the course of his short life he cultivated a massive correspondence, becoming perhaps the single greatest producer of letters in the world. His personal philosophy toward life in general and specifically fiction writing was that of the amateur gentleman who dabbled at a hobby.

Most of what he was paid for was revision writing—taking material of less talented authors and "ghostwriting" it so that it became suitable for submission to a professional market—which he did with some reluctance and only to purchase the meager amount of food for his table and the considerable amount of postage for his correspondence. Once he turned down the offer of Editorship of *Weird Tales*, the pulp that would later make his name famous, for fear of becoming a professional.

Ironically, despite Lovecraft's best efforts to remain obscure, many of the concepts he invented later influenced a school of writers, and, indeed, laid the groundwork for a major sub-formula of the supernatural genre: dark fantasy.

Lovercraft's first published story for *Weird Tales*, "Dagon" (1917), offers a touchstone for the examination of the dark fantasy sub-formula, as well as a sociological vehicle for the reflection of a post-World War I American society and outlines a cognitive attitude toward various institutions that, in part, affected reality construction and philosophical attitudes.

Like a good deal of Lovecraft's fiction, "Dagon" is narrated in the first person. Unnamed, the narrator simply describes himself as a "supercargo" of a freight ship sailing in the Pacific during World War I. In typical Lovecraftian manner, the sailor begins his narrative with the action of the adventure already concluded. A powerful sense of doom pervades the story as the sailor/narrator begins his tale stating that he is under an "appreciable mental strain" since his supply of drugs is running out and he is without means to purchase more. He threatens suicide to relieve his plight, yet admonishes the reader that he is not a weakling or a degenerate. He offers his adventure to the reader in the guise of "hastily scrawled pages," and indirectly implores the reader to become his confessor ... and perhaps his judge.

The above literary device, borrowed from the Victorian method of framing a story so that distance, objectivity and a greater sense of realism are achieved, accomplishes two things. First, since the story will be requiring the reader to suspend his disbelief of the events of the narrator's adventure, this framing device allows a certain verisimilitude to creep in. And second, since the narrator has already informed the reader that he is doomed, a mood is quickly established and a guidepost erected informing the reader that the *process*, rather than the *result*, of the narration is of central interest. The sign on the guidepost reads, "this is not a happy ending for the hero of the story," and the reader is duly prepared to expect the worst.

Like the Gothic romance, the tale of dark fantasy established a formulaic confrontation that pits the individual against the greater forces of the cosmos. But in the Gothic romance, as the individual recognizes his precarious position in the larger scheme of things, and is perhaps killed by certain transgressions (i.e., the villain perverting sexual taboos, in-group murder), the protagonist representing the larger society learns from these transgressions and further respects the powers of the cosmos via the traditions of institutions. The protagonist in the dark fantasy formula, usually represented by Lovecraft as a scholar (an archeologist, professor or world traveler), as he investigates the mysteries of life and of the cosmos itself is totally destroyed. There is no human agent acting as villain, only a collection of elemental forces that represent total evil in the sense that they act extremely hostile toward humanity and literally lie in wait for that poor unfortunate who crosses the line from blissful ignorance to damning knowledge. Such a formula suggests a sociological assumption, reinforcing perhaps the most reactionary attitude towards certain beliefs.

As Lovecraft's narrator in "Dagon" (the sailor or world traveler protagonist) is stranded on the seas of the "broad Pacific" (ironically not "pacific" at all) he recognizes his uncertain fate in the midst of a greater elemental force, and begins to "despair in [his] solitude upon the heaving vastness of unbroken blue."[23] The sociological implication here advocates a respect for ignorance, and indeed recommends strong restraint for the person who abandons the social group in quest for cosmic truth. Nature, as the symbol of force (and as an agent of death and destruction), is best left to itself.

As the sea reveals its secrets to the sailor/narrator, in a cataclysm that heaves the bottom of the ocean to the surface, and as the impulse for knowledge strikes when he discovers a "well-shaped monolith whose massive bulk had known the workmanship and perhaps the worship of living and thinking creatures,"[24] the final breach between ignorance and knowledge, between tradition and science, is transgressed and a new reality is unveiled; the narrator/sailor's destruction is sealed; and part of that agent of the newly discovered reality is language:

Across the chasm, the wavelets washed the base of the Cyclopean monolith, on whose surface I could now trace both inscriptions and crude sculptures. The writing was in a system of hieroglyphics unknown to me, and unlike anything I had ever seen in books .... Awestruck at this unexpected glimpse into a past beyond the conception of the most daring anthropologist, I stood musing whilst the moon cast queer reflections on the silent channel before me.[25]

Lovecraft's implementation of language as a device that bridges the "chasm" of ignorance ironically recognizes the power of language as a sociological tool for the construction of reality. In people's culture, language is part of a socialization process that assists the discrete identification of objects and social roles. For Lovecraft, and dark fantasy writers in general, the language socializer functions as a motif of horror, if one reads what one is not supposed to read.

Lovecraft's narrator/sailor quickly dismisses his anthropological joy in new discovery as he next views the agent of the hieroglyphics, a "Polyphemus-like" creature, a "stupendous monster of nightmares," which rises from the dark waters, a view which drives him insane. He survives the experience, ending up in a hospital in San Francisco. At a loss to explain his vision, he attributes the horror as being "the ancient Philistine legend of Dagon, the Fish-God."[26] As the tale concludes, the narrator/sailor prophesies the day when the monsters of the deep sea will rise to the surface to drag humanity down, and then promptly describes his own destruction, whether actual or imagined: "...the end is near. I hear a noise at the door, as of some immense slippery body lumbering against it. It shall not find me. God *that hand*! The window! The window!"[27]

Using many of the motifs first developed in "Dagon" and other early efforts, Lovecraft would later evolve a series of loosely interconnected stories termed by critics the Cthulhu Mythos. The Cthulhu Mythos further expanded Lovecraft's dark vision of humanity and further solidified the position of dark fantasy within the supernatural formula. Perhaps no other single literary creation has been so influential in motivating young and veteran authors in extending and elaborating the scope of the supernatural vision as has Lovecraft's Mythos cycle, inspiring such popular horror writers as Robert E. Howard, Clark Ashton Smith, Robert Bloch, Ramsey Campbell, Colin Wilson, Brian Lumley, Stephen King and August Derleth. And the sociological motivation that centers as the driving force behind this legion of pastiches and imitators is the collective fear, a paranoiac fear, if you will, of those very symbols in our society that advocate civilization and progress: language, science, rational inquiry into Natural phenomena. Dark fantasy parallels the other sub-formulas of supernatural fiction in that it places the individual within cognitive references of good and evil. The actions of the individual on earth have their parallel with actions in heaven and hell.[28] The structure of the conflict of supernatural fiction between God and the Devil presents a working model for the individual. People can identify their institutions as having a divine parallel, and thus these institutions gain the force of sacred power.[29] Denial of that power can embody a type of divine intervention, for the betterment or for the destruction, of human action.

The dark fantasy sub-formula was an outgrowth of, and reaction to, World War I. Unlike any other conflict in the history of humankind, World War I involved more nations, more people and caused more death and destruction (especially to innocent civilians) than had its predecessors. And the single greatest catalyst that assisted humanity in this wholesale slaughter was technology: new weapons, better weapons, weapons like poison gas and the tank and the machine gun and the flame-thrower, devices of death that destroyed not hundreds of lives, but thousands. After an assessment was made at the conclusion of the war of the human cost, technology (and the progenitors of technology: science, rationality and knowledge) began to be perceived as potentially uncontrollable if handled by the wrong people. Dark fantasy thus exemplifies a rather conservative perspective of world maintenance (as had other "modern" art forms, like Dadaism and Abstraction). The seeker of information, of knowledge, of a science that is not meant to be known, in dark fantasy fiction is defined within the frame of the sub-formula as a social deviant, a type of "scientific heretic." The world maintenance function of dark fantasy exemplifies the physical and/or spiritual destruction of these deviant individuals, since the successful completion of the "heretic's" scientific experiments would result in worldwide havoc. And though the scientific heretic is consumed by the demonic agencies he seeks to contact (and inadvertently release upon the world) before the "worst" happens, the message of the tale remains clear: those demons are out there still, just beyond the individual's vision, waiting for the right person to release them at the right time. It would be another "war" in which divine forces *do* impinge upon the lives of people, and in which no individual wins.

The Emergence of the Psycho-Killer

The literary groundwork was laid for the psycho-killer sub-formula by James Hogg's *The Private Memoirs and Confessions of a Justified Sinner* (1824), the first example in popular fiction of the split-personality. Hogg (1770-1835) was a Scottish poet and was successful in incorporating supernatural elements of oral folktales told to him by his mother in his short fiction (twenty-two of which were collected in his book *Winter's Evening Tales*, 1820), thus creating the illusion of "home-spun" storytelling. His most significant work, however, was not his poetry nor his short stories but an interestingly structured novel; *The Private Memoirs and Confessions of a Justified Sinner* is divided into two sections: a tale narrated by the editor and a tale narrated by the "sinner." Part I of Hogg's novel tells of the conflict between two half-brothers and the eventual murder of the one brother by the other. Part II is told from the point-of-view of Robert Wringhim, Jr. (the murderer of

Part I) and describes the seduction of Wringhim by the mysterious Gil-Martin (Wringhim's "look-alike"). Over time, Wringhim begins to suspect what the reader already knows, that Gil-Martin is really the Devil in disguise, but is nonetheless persuaded by Gil-Martin to commit a number of murders. Wringhim soon is stricken with amnesia; the killings continue with Wringhim believing that Gil-Martin is responsible. Eventually, Wringhim relinquishes more and more of his personality to Gil-Martin's control and tries to flee from his demon "double." Gil-Martin finally convinces Wringhim to take his own life, and the tale ends with the narrator being discovered in the grave of a suicide with a hay rope tied around his neck.[30]

Since the publication of Hogg's novel a number of novels have worked with the split-personality motif complex, Robert Louis Stevenson's *The Strange Case of Dr. Jekyll and Mr. Hyde* (1888) being perhaps the most famous example. But it wasn't until the publication of Robert Bloch's *Psycho* that the split-personality motif complex coalesced into the psycho-killer variant of the supernatural story. Bloch (1917-) was an avid reader of pulp magazines during his youth. He was especially fond of *Weird Tales*, and he later became a contributor to the magazine with such short stories as "Lilies" (1934), a story about an old woman who continues to deliver flowers after her death, and "The Secret in the Tomb" (1935), a grisly tale concerning a man whose ancestor was a ghoul.[31] During his early years as a writer of horror fiction, Bloch was a fan and correspondent of H.P. Lovecraft, and much of his work during this period shows a distinctly Lovecraftian influence. Over time, as Bloch developed his skills, he moved away from the Lovecraft brand of dark fantasy and started exploring new territories in the supernatural formula with his novels *The Scarf* (1947), *The Kidnapper* (1954) and *The Will to Kill* (1954). By *Psycho* (1959) Bloch had hit his stride, creating a type of fiction that was later to influence profoundly the direction not only of contemporary supernatural novels and short stories but contemporary horror films as well. Alfred Hitchcock's faithful adaptation of *Psycho*, for example, was so popular that it generated a score of imitations in the 1950s, 1960s and 1970s, including the Carpenter *Halloween* films and the numerous *Friday the 13th* movies.

Psycho draws the Gothic tradition to a conclusion with Bloch's use of the sexual variety of the human-inspired aberration of nature. Norman Bates (his first name a pun on the word normal), the protagonist of the story, is described at the start as a son dominated by his mother. The one side of Norman's personality loves reassurance and orderliness, which he finds in the house that he has lived in for forty years with his mother. But there is a dark side to Norman, which is nicely underscored by Bloch in the first chapter. Norman is sitting in his home, reading Victor W. Von Hagen's *The Realm of the Incas,* when he comes across the section illustrating the Inca *cachua,* or victory dance, where the body of an enemy is flayed and the belly streteched to form a drum:

It wasn't the most appetizing notion in the world, but when Norman closed his eyes, he could almost see the scene: this throng of painted, naked warriors wriggling and swaying in unison under a sun-drenched, savage sky, and the old crone crouching before them, throbbing out a relentless rhythm on the swollen, distended belly of a cadaver. The contorted mouth of the corpse would be forced open, probably fixed in a gaping grimace by clamps of bone, and from it the sound emerged . . . .[32]

This passage causes Norman to have a comfortable shiver, suggesting that he is both attracted and fascinated by grotesque violence (implied by Bloch's word choice of "comfortable"). Norman's mother interrupts his reading and harps on the poor business that their motel is doing (the motel being next to their house) since a new road has diverted most of the traffic away. Norman looks at the house about him, and reveals to the reader that he hates the "long familiarity . . . of the objects in the room . . . like the furnishings of a prison cell."[33] This love/hate attitude extends to his mother also, and with his discovery that there is no escape from the house (or from his mother, Bloch suggests), a voice throbs in his head: "the voice that drummed into his ears [was] like that of the Inca corpse in the book; the drum of the dead."[34] As the argument rages between Norman and his mother, the hint of sexual perversion creeps in with Norman's mother commenting on the Von Hagen book: " 'And I'll bet it's crammed full of nasty bits about those savages, like the one you had about the South Seas? Oh, you didn't think I knew about *that* one did you? Hiding it up in your room, the way you hid all the others, those filthy things you used to read—' "[35] Norman tries to explain that his reading deals with psychology, and tells his mother about the "Oedipus situation," hoping that she will understand their relationship. She doesn't, of course, which later proves ironic since their problem is Oedipal and psychological, but not as Norman understands it.

Bloch shifts the attention of the novel in the second chapter to Mary Crane, a clerk who steals forty-thousand dollars from her place of employment, the Lowery Agency, so that she can finally marry her boyfriend Sam Loomis. Mary is on the run, hoping that her employer won't notice the theft until she is long gone. She takes a wrong turn on the road, and ends up at the Bates motel:

She switched off the ignition and waited. All at once she could hear the sullen
patter of the rain and sense the sigh of the wind behind it. She remembered the
sound, because it had rained like that the day Mom was buried, the day they
lowered her into that little rectangle of darkness. And now the darkness was
here, rising all around Mary. She was alone in the dark. The money wouldn't
help her and Sam wouldn't help her, because she'd taken the wrong turn back
there and she was on a strange road. But no help for it—she made her grave and
now she must lie in it.... [36]

Indeed, she *has* made her grave (as Bloch puns) by stealing and by being
lost in moral darkness, and Fate *does* make her lie in it. Mary meets
Norman, and signs up for a room at his motel. He invites her up to the
house for a snack. While there, Norman tells Mary about his hobby,
taxidermy (another clue to Norman's character), and Mary asks if he
hunts. He replies that his mother doesn't want him to handle firearms,
to which Mary says: " 'You certainly must realize that you can't be
expected to act like a little boy all the rest of your life,' "[37] suggesting
further that Norman's mother should be put in an "institution."
Norman reacts in a rage, claiming that his mother is not crazy and that
he owes her for taking care of him for all these years and retorting:
" 'But who are you to say a person should be put away? I think all of us
go a little crazy at times.' "[38] Norman calms down, but Mary senses
something about Norman: " 'He is afraid to touch me...the poor
guy is actually afraid to get near a woman!' "[39]

Mary returns to the motel and prepares to take a shower. She decides
to return the money, her conscience getting the better of her, and feels
good about her decision, thinking:

If she'd been a religious girl she would have prayed. As it was, she felt a curious
sense of—what was that word?—predestination. As if everything that had
happened was somehow fated to be. Her turning off on the wrong road, coming
here, meeting that pathetic man, listening to his outburst, hearing that final
sentence which brought her to her senses.... [40]

Mary then undresses to take a shower. Again, Bloch describes the scene
in a restrained manner, spending only a paragraph on it, but in that
paragraph he reveals a voyeuristic insight into Mary's young sexuality:

For the moment she stood before the mirror set in the door and took stock of
herself. Maybe the face was twenty-seven, but the body was free, white and
twenty-one. She had a good figure. A damned good figure. Sam would like it.
She wished he was here to admire it now. It was going to be hell to wait another

two years. But then she'd make up for lost time. They say a woman isn't fully mature, sexually, until she's thirty. That was something to find out about....[41]

Of course Mary never has the chance to find out about her sexual maturity, since she is promptly murdered in the shower by a figure with a face powdered dead white: "the face of a crazy old woman."[42]

The balance of *Psycho* deals with Norman's attempts to cover up Mary's murder—which he thinks his mother committed—and the follow-up investigation of Mary's theft by a private detective, Milton Arbogast, who is murdered by the "female" killer as he gets too close to the truth. Lila, Mary's sister, also wants to know about the fate of her sister and persuades Sam Loomis to help her, following Mary's trail to the Bates' motel. The climax of the story comes when Lila and Sam learn from the local sheriff that Norman's mother has been dead for years (and the reader learns that Norman himself is responsible for the killings). The reader, as "detective," surmises that Norman is the psycho-killer, and Bloch further develops the suspense of the novel as he moves Lila and Sam to the scene of the crimes, placing Lila in mortal danger. While in the basement of the Bates' home, she encounters the killer:

Lila turned to stare at the fat, shapeless figure, half-concealed by the tight dress which had been pulled down incongruously to cover the garments beneath. She stared up at the shrouding shawl, and at the white, painted, simpering face beneath it. She stared at the garishly reddened lips, watched them part in a convulsive grimace .... "I am Norma Bates, said the high, shrill voice...."[43]

Norman/Norma attacks Lila with a knife, but Lila is saved by Sam who grabs Norman and wrests the knife from his hand. Bloch uses the final chapter to postulate a psychological motive for Norman's behavior. Dr. Steiner, Norman's psychiatrist, explains to Sam and Lila that Norman was a transvestite who impersonated his dead mother (who had so dominated him as a child and whom he had murdered when he learned that she was about to leave him after falling in love with another man): " 'In a way, Norman wanted to be like his mother, and in a way he wanted his mother to become a part of himself.' "[44] Norman had thus become psychotic:

"There was *Norman*, the little boy who needed his mother and hated anything or anyone who came between him and her. Then *Norma*, the mother, who could not be allowed to die. The third aspect might be called *Normal*—the adult Norman Bates, who had to go through the daily routine of living, and conceal the existence of the other personalities from the world...."[45]

Norman's psychosis extended to his necrophiliac desire to preserve the body of his dead mother, as well as her personality, and so he robbed her grave, stuffed her, dressed her, and carried her body through the motions of a pseudo-life.

Bloch's manipulation of the sexual human-inspired aberration of nature functions at two levels. The author has often remarked that his inspiration for *Psycho* came from a highly publicized, gruesome murder case—the Ed Gein killings near Plainsfield, Wisconsin in the late 1950s. Gein not only murdered his victims, he slaughtered them, using pieces of their bodies to furnish his farm, ate them and adorned himself with parts of his victims' female anatomy. Thus, *Psycho* as a fictional testament of "real life" sexual perversion, investigates, at one level, the social mechanism of "abnormality." The concept of deviance occurs when legitimized programs of action are defied or denied, thus threatening the continuation of social order. Society imposes sanctions upon deviant behavior in order to insure its own survival. Hence individuals are taught to stay in line, or else.... [46] *Psycho*, and other psycho-killer popular fiction, is a literary exploration of the sexual abnormality aspect of deviance. Norman's behavior is deviant because he: 1) develops an overt, unhealthy (both personally and socially) sexual relationship with his mother; 2) defies the physical and social boundaries of "maleness" and "femaleness" by dressing and acting like his mother; and 3) destructively expresses his sexual abnormality through terrible, violent acts. *Psycho* operates as a sanction itself, by allowing the reader to examine the horrors of Norman's crimes and by encouraging speculation of the "positive" values of compliance to incest and in-group murder taboos. On another level, with regard to the formulaic structure of the psycho-killer story, *Psycho* defines the conflict between the individual and his sexuality and violence. Though technically possessing no supernatural motif complexes, the psycho-killer story falls within the supernatural formula because of the relationship between the individual and Fate, with Fate "ordaining" violent death that seems to have no rational justification for its existence. In the Gothic tale, people confront the world, and the forces of supernature keep them in their place. In supernatural and dark fantasy tales, people confront physical manifestations of supernature, and the negative side of supernature—evil—which kill or subdue them. In the psycho-killer story, people are their own worst monsters, their own killers, their own destroyers, and hence the conflict of this type of story is between people and their own abnormality. The sexual nature of the psycho-killer's abnormality presents a choice of sorts, allowing the individual to choose standards of reality definition, in fact demanding a choice.[47] Specifically, in *Psycho*, the author by demonstrating the socially negative results of Norman's behavior implies that a positive reality *can* be achieved if Norman (or the normal person) acts the way "a person should act" (which means that he should not communicate his "sexual hang-ups" with a butcher knife). "Evil" Fate can be avoided if a positive reality is constructed, just as vampires of the supernatural story can be avoided if the power icons of religion are employed (like the cross).

Notes

[1]Martin Kallich, *Horace Walpole* (New York: Twayne, 1971), p. 101.

[2]Devendra P. Varma, *The Gothic Flame* (London: Arthur Barker, 1957), pp. 10-11.

[3]Horace Walpole, *The Castle of Otranto: A Gothic Story* (London: Oxford University Press, 1964), p. 15.

[4]*Ibid.*, p. 32.

[5]*Ibid.*, p. 25.

[6]Peter L. Berger and Thomas Luckmann, *The Social Construction of Reality* (Garden City: Doubleday, 1966), p. 95.

[7]Walpole, p. 23.

[8]*Ibid.*

[9]Peter L. Berger, *The Sacred Canopy: Elements of A Sociological Theory of Religion* (Garden City: Doubleday, 1967), p. 39.

[10]Walpole, p. 108.

[11]Berger, p. 23.

[12]John Polidori, "The Vampyre," *Vampires at Midnight*, Peter Haining, ed., (New York: Gosset & Dunlap, 1970), p. 29.

[13]*Ibid.*, p. 30.

[14]Berger, p. 59.

[15]*Ibid.*

[16]Polidori, p. 26.

[17]*Ibid.*, p.40.

[18]*Ibid.*, p. 41.

[19]Berger, p. 61.

[20]*Ibid.*

[21]Polidori, p. 37.

[22]Berger, p. 39.

[23]H.P. Lovecraft, "Dagon," *Dagon and Other Macabre Tales* (Sauk City: Arkham House, 1965), p. 3.

[24]*Ibid.*, p. 6.

[25]*Ibid.*

[26]*Ibid.*, p. 7.

[27]*Ibid.*, p. 8.

[28]Berger, p. 34.

[29]*Ibid.*

[30]Ann B. Tracy, *The Gothic Novel: 1790-1830* (Lexington: The University of Kentucky Press, 1981), pp. 72-73.

[31]Mike Ashley, *Who's Who in Horror and Fantasy Fiction* (New York: Taplinger, 1977), p. 38.

[32]Robert Bloch, *Psycho* (New York: Bantam Books, 1959), p. 2.
[33]*Ibid.*, p. 5.
[34]*Ibid.*
[35]*Ibid.*, p. 6.
[36]*Ibid.*, p. 17.
[37]*Ibid.*, p. 23.
[38]Ibid., p. 24.
[39]*Ibid.*, p. 25.
[40]*Ibid.*, p. 27.
[41]*Ibid.*, pp. 27-28.
[42]*Ibid.*, p. 28.
[43]*Ibid.*, p. 127.
[44]*Ibid.*, p. 127.
[45]*Ibid.*, pp. 132-133.
[46]Berger and Luckmann, p. 62.
[47]*Ibid.*, p. 168.

CHAPTER IV
Fiction Noir Formula

The Light Angel: Cornell Woolrich and Urban Alienation
RESIDING NEXT TO THE SUPERNATURAL formula at the Irrational end of the mystery genre spectrum is the fiction noir sub-formula. The fiction noir story saw its start in that transitional phase between the dime novel and the pulp magazine. 1915 was a significant year in the development of entertainment print mass media, for it witnessed the transformation of one of the last dime novel holdouts, *Nick Carter Stories*, into the first pulp magazine (or any popular publication for that matter) to entirely feature mystery fiction: Street and Smith's *Detective Story Magazine*.[1] As with today's mass paperback industry, commercial success bred imitation, and soon there followed scores of crime and detective fiction magazines, including *The Black Mask*, *Flynn's Weekly Detective Fiction* (the title later changed to *Detective Fiction Weekly*), *Detective Dragnet* (the title later changed to *Ten Detective Aces*), *Ace Detective*, *Thrilling Detective*, *Clues*, *Popular Detective*, *Super Detective* and the list goes on and on. Nearly all the formulas of mystery fiction were either first created or refined in the American pulp magazines of the 1920s and 1930s. And their continued financial health and proliferation of numbers during this period created a collection of mystery story forms, among them, the fiction noir formula.

Despite their many shortcomings (i.e., lack of characterization, rigid length requirements for individual stories, low pay for the authors and high profit for the publisher), the pulps, and specifically the mystery pulps, forced their authors to "streamline" their writing, the result being a paradigmatic shift in the way popular fiction was created. For example, pulp magazine publishers, in order to insure high profits (and in order to remain competitive), successfully utilized the fiction factory method (as first developed in the dime novels) to mass produce their product. From the author's vantage, the only way to make a living in the fiction factory system was to "manufacture" as much writing as he physically could, and the only way in which he could muster this high level of production was to streamline his work. Streamlining thus changed the form of popular fiction in three ways: 1) The process of writing was speeded up (so that more stories could be produced) by eliminating descriptive adjectives, by shortening the length of the sentences and by simplifying the language. 2) More conversation was employed to relate the narrative since this reduced the need to spend time fleshing out detailed plot, character and setting structures. 3) And most importantly (for the mystery pulps), pulp writers turned to material that was literally at their fingertips—the city streets, which thus provided them with endless topics that could be easily assimilated in their work. The American mystery pulps of the 1920s and 1930s became a vehicle for the expression of an urban vernacular, a vernacular that embodied collective anxieties of city life. The dominant anxiety of this urban vernacular, alienation, was extensively explored in the pulp mystery hard-boiled sub-formula (which will be discussed in Chapter 8) and the fiction noir formula.

Cornell (George Hopley) Woolrich (1903-1968) was among the first to establish the motif complexes of the fiction noir story. Starting in 1934, Woolrich abandoned his attempts at becoming another F. Scott Fitzgerald and ceased writing his Fitzgeraldian pastiches, mainstream novels like *Cover Charge* (1926), *Children of the Ritz* (1927) and *Time Square* (1929), and began selling fiction to the mystery pulps. This change of literary direction seemed to have coincided with the advent of the Great Depression in America. Woolrich's writing entered into a dark phase which was quite a departure from his earlier work. Foremost Woolrich scholar, Francis M. Nevins, Jr., nicely canvasses this new phrase:

Although he [Woolrich] wrote many types of stories, including quasi-police procedural novels, rapid-action whizbangs, and tales of the occult, Woolrich is best known as the master of pure suspense, evoking with awesome power the desperation of those who walk the city's darkened streets and the terror that lurks at noonday in commonplace settings. In his hands even such cliched storylines as the race to save the innocent man from the electric chair and the amnesiac's search for his lost self resonate with human anguish. Woolrich's world is a feverish place where the prevailing emotions are loneliness and fear and the prevailing action a race against time and death, as in his suspense classics "Three O'Clock" and "Guillotine." His most characteristic detective stories end with our realization that no rational account of events is possible, and his suspense stories tend to close not with the dissipation of the terror but with its omnipresence.[2]

Woolrich used the pulps as a "proving ground" to hone his writing skills, and in 1940 he started publishing hardcover novels, his "Black" series—including *The Bride Wore Black* (1940), *The Black Curtain* (1941), *Black Alibi* (1942), *The Black Angel* (1943) and *The Black Path of Fear* (1944)—which later became Hollywood's cinematic model for a number of crime films produced in the 1940s and 1950s, and termed film noir ("dark" film) by French film critics. The conclusion to Woolrich's life was as bleak as anything he ever wrote. Suffering from repressed homosexuality and a domineering mother, he died in misery of an infection resulting from an amputated gangrenous leg, living his final years confined to a wheelchair and consumed by alcoholism, diabetes and self-hate.[3]

Woolrich's short story "Angel Face" (first published as "Face Work" in the October, 1937 issue of *Black Mask*), though not his first effort in the mystery pulps, is one of his earliest works to encompass the two major motif complexes of the fiction (also termed "roman") noir formula: the light/dark angel and urban alienation.

The protagonist of "Angel Face" is Jerry Wheeler, a woman of great beauty (hence her nickname: Angel Face), intelligence and courage. But she also has a "bad" past. "I've been around plenty," Jerry tells her brother, Chick, "and, around wasn't pretty."[4] Jerry's earlier life in the "gutter," rather than destroying her, has instead given her an inner moral strength and an insight into the personality of others. As the story opens, Jerry is at the apartment of her brother's girlfriend. She is pleading with Ruby Rose Reading to leave her brother alone: "He's just a man, doesn't know what's good for him, doesn't know his bass from his oboe .... Pick on someone your size, someone that can take it. Have your fun and more power to you—but not with all I've got."[5] Ruby laughs at Jerry Wheeler, and replies: " 'I've heard of wives pulling this act, and even mothers, and in a pitcher I saw only lately, Camilly it was called, it was the old man. Now it's a sister .... Send grandma around tomorrow—next week East Lynne.' "[6] Ruby is a hard woman, a heart-breaker, a man-killer, who uses sex to get what she wants as easily as other women use a towel to dry their hands. Though residing in an expensive apartment, she has bad taste, eating a "pink soda-fountain mess" for breakfast when first talking to Jerry; later demanding her maid to " 'take Foo-Too around the block a couple of times' " (only a "tramp" owns a dog named Foo-Too, Woolrich implies). In just these first few paragraphs, Woolrich has delineated the fiction noir motif complex of the light/dark angel by giving the reader an example of each with these two women in conflict. Jerry, as the light angel, is compassionate, deeply caring for her brother, and willing to go to any lengths to protect him (as we shall see). Despite her sordid past and her ability to manipulate men with her sexual charms, she only does so to protect her loved ones. Ruby Rose Reading, on the other hand, employs sex to destroy men, as she intends to do with Jerry's brother. She is a monster, a destroyer, and she takes great pleasure in hurting others. Both Jerry and Ruby are cynical, but Jerry has risen above her cynicism, dispatching it, while Ruby has not. Jerry's character offers an interesting social comment, as emblematic of fiction noir's light angel, on the "bad woman turned good" (or the "whore with a heart of gold"). People are capable of almost any manner of sexual aberration. However, human sexuality is directed by institutions in every society.[7] Jerry has participated in non-sanctioned sexual misconduct, so to speak, but she has learned from her experience, changed herself, and striven to use her "knowledge" to help others. She presents an example of how to control sexual lust, and how to channel human desire into positive or "good" areas. The "evil" side of lust, the domain of the dark angel, shall be discussed later in this chapter. The light angel is a "savior" figure ultimately, who, undergoing the "sin-suffering-salvation" process, heals the rest of us.

After Ruby Rose Reading rebuffs her plea, Jerry turns to her brother and demands that he leave this evil woman alone. Chick's response is to strike Jerry to the floor and leave her to go take Ruby away to Chicago with him. Later, two police detectives visit Jerry at her apartment. They tell her that they have Chick for the murder of Ruby, and present their circumstantial evidence:

"I've been on the squad eight years now. We never in all that time caught a guy dead to rights as your brother. He showed up with his valise in the foyer of the Alcazar at exactly twelve minutes past eight tonight. He said to the doorman, 'What time is it? Did Miss Reading send her baggage out yet? We've got to make a train;' Well, she had sent her baggage down and then she'd changed her mind, she'd had it all taken back upstairs again. There's your motive right there. The doorman rang her apartment and said through the announcer, 'Mr. Wheeler's here.' And she gave a dirty laugh and sang out, 'I can hardly wait.'

"So at thirteen past eight she was still alive. He went up, and he's no sooner got there than her apartment began to signal the doorman frantically. No one answered his hail over the announcer, so he chased up, and he found your brother crouched over her, shaking her and she was dead. At fifteen minutes past eight o'clock. Is that a case or is that a case...."[8]

Chick is tried and convicted of the murder of Ruby, but Jerry is compelled by love to try and save her brother from execution. One of the two detectives who visited Jerry at her apartment, Nick Burns, feels sorry (and perhaps love) for Jerry, and tells her:

"Sell me, won't you?" .... "Sell me that he's innocent, and I'll work my fingers raw to back you up. I didn't frame your brother. I only did my job. I was sent there by my superiors in answer to the patrolman's call that night, questioned Chick, put him under arrest .... Don't hold that against me Angel Face...."[9]

Jerry, with Nick Burns' help, plays detective to track down the real killer, who turns out to be a Greek gangster named Militis. As the light angel, she uses her sex appeal to seduce Militis and acquire the evidence she needs to prevent her brother's "date" with the electric chair. She finally succeeds, almost dying in the attempt after Militis discovers that she is Chick's sister, and she proves to Nick that the Greek had "set up" Chick for Ruby's killing. Militis was one of Ruby's boyfriends, and when he learned that she was going to leave town with another man, he murdered her and used Chick as the fall guy.

The plot of "Angel Face" is one of Woolrich's favorites: the race against time to save life. Chick Wheeler is a victim of Fate in the story, an innocent victim who demonstrates almost total lack of control of the events of his life. He is manipulated by the dark angel figure, Ruby, into deserting his sister. He is arrested, and convicted, for Ruby's murder—a crime he did not commit. He is sentenced to die in the electric chair. His only means of escape from this grim Fate is through his sister's help, and she must race against time to get her brother acquitted before it is too late. In the fiction noir formula, though Fate does not manifest itself in the mortal world via supernatural means (as it does, say, in the Gothic), it nonetheless represents a force that is greater than the individual's. For Chick in "Angel Face," Fate is masked in the guise of the "system," the police who arrest him because it is "their job," the courts who convict him because of the overwhelming evidence laid against him. The fact that he is innocent is meaningless. Fate, illustrated by Chick's helplessness when confronted by the urban system (its police, courts and laws), is a formulaic presentation, in the fiction noir story, of the urban alienation motif complex. Alienation can be defined sociologically as the loss of meaning between the individual and his socially created world.[10] The system in "Angel Face" is human-made (the courts, the laws), but as an alienating factor, it has "escaped" his control. Thus, the system has lost its meaning for its creator and the individual finds himself a stranger within that system (and a stranger to himself).[11] Since the system is housed in the city, governed by the city, the city functions in the fiction noir formula as the primary alienating factor. It is a place alien and dangerous to the individual, where those rules and regulations that should normally protect the individual's safety and happiness otherwise act to destroy that safety and happiness, if certain conditions are met, as we shall see outlined in the following section.

Sex and the Dark Angel: James M. Cain and Urban Alienation

The first, and perhaps strongest, example of the dark angel motif complex in the fiction noir formula appears in James M. Cain's *The Postman Always Rings Twice* (1934). And without the mediating influence of a light angel savior figure, Cain's short novel chronicles the implacable consequences of human lust "gone wrong."

The Postman Always Rings Twice was Cain's first published novel, and he held a long and productive career as a writer, publishing such critically acclaimed works as *Serenade* (1937), *Mildred Pierce* (1941), *Three of a Kind: Career in C Major, The Embezzler, Double Indemnity* (1943) and *The Butterfly* (1947). James M. Cain (1892-1977) had once stated that he belonged "to no school, hard-boiled or otherwise" of popular fiction,[12] yet a great amount of his creative work deals with crime and violence. Discussing this aspect of Cain's writing, critic John S. Whitley states:

Cain rarely writes mystery novels (perhaps only *Jealous Woman* properly comes into this category) so that murder and crime become, in his work, not something which can be solved and hence disposed of in a cleansing motion, but part of the unalterable series of events usually set in motion by a meeting between man and woman which can exert the same relentless grip (on both protagonists and readers) as Fate in Greek tragedy or Chance in the novels of Thomas Hardy. Part of Cain's power comes from his ability to show the fragility of order and common-sense.[13]

The impact of Cain's narration of the relationship between the individual and Fate (emblematic in fiction noir of alienation) in *The Postman Always Rings Twice* later influenced Camus' writing of his novel *The Stranger*, and the subsequent development of the existential philosophical tradition, hence showing Cain to be one of the foremost storytellers in American popular literature.[14]

As the story opens in *The Postman Always Rings Twice*, the reader is introduced to the road tramp, Frank Chambers. Frank is an amoral protagonist, having led a life "on the edge" of being evil as the following dialogue between Chambers and Sackett, a District Attorney (who is holding Frank on a murder charge) illustrates mid-way into the novel. When asked by Sackett about his past, Frank says:

"Oh, knocked around?"

"Hitch-hiked? Rode freights? Bummed your meals wherever you could?"

"Yes, sir."

He [Sackett] unstrapped a briefcase, put a pile of papers on the table, and began looking through them. "Ever been in Frisco?"

"Born there."

"Kansas City? New York? New Orleans? Chicago?"

"I've seen them all."

"Ever been in jail?"

"I have, judge. You knock around, you get in trouble with the cops now and then. Yes sir, I've been in jail."

"Ever been in jail in Tucson?"

"Yes, sir, I think it was ten days I got there. It was for trespassing on railroad property."

"Salt Lake City? San Diego? Wichita?"

"Yes sir. All those places."

"Oakland?"

"I got three months there, judge. I got in a fight with a railroad detective."

"You beat him up pretty bad, didn't you?"

"Well, as the fellow says, he was beat up pretty bad, but you ought to have seen the other one. I was beat up pretty bad, myself."[15]

But Frank is a likeable fellow, and as he is kicked off a hay truck on which he has stolen a ride at the start of the first chapter, the truckers (rather than "roughing him up" or turning him into the police) give him a cigarette. Despite his past Frank possesses the gift of freedom, total freedom. He goes where he wants, when he wants, and is answerable for his actions to no power. Frank also, however, possesses two faults, both of which eventually bring on his doom: violence and sexual lust. After being thrown from the hay truck, Frank enters a "roadside sandwich joint," the Twin Oaks Tavern, where he is offered a breakfast by the owner, a Greek named Nick Papadakis. Nick offers Frank a job at the restaurant, which Frank promises to "think about," exercising his freedom to choose (his free will), that is, until he sees "her," Cain's dark angel, the female man-killer, the destroyer of freedom and the weaver of Frank's trap—Cora, Nick's wife.

When Frank first looks at Cora, he describes her as no "raving beauty," but he is fatally attracted to her "sultry look" anyway, seeing "her lips stuck out in a way that made [him] want to mash them in for her."[16] His lust for Cora starting to overcome him, Frank stays on at Nick's restaurant waiting for his chance to get near her. Frank's first extended conversation with Cora is structured by Cain as a verbal "fighting match." Cora starts the match by telling Frank that she is not a "Mex" and that she is as "white" as he is (an interesting use of the word white, since she and Frank are anything but morally pure). Frank recognizes Cora's vulnerable dilemma (her marriage to the non-white Greek) and throws his counter-punch by asking why she married Nick. Cora jumps at Frank's question, as if he had "cut her with a whip" (another phrase of violence), responding: " 'Is that any of your business?' " His counter-punch is a knockout blow:

> I had what I wanted. I had socked one in under her guard, and socked it in deep, so it hurt. From now on, it would be business between her and me. She might not say yes, but she wouldn't stall me. She knew what I meant, and she knew I had her number.[17]

Nick, of course, is oblivious to the steam rising from the sexual lust generated between Frank and his wife. He likes Frank, wanting him to stay around, thinking it a "great victory" when Frank eats well at his place. But the animal nature in Frank is consuming him, driving his lust, as he begins to "smell" Cora as she works about him, and his lust starts to dominate his being: "It was like hell, the lunch, or the potatoes, or the wine," Frank tells his reader. "I wanted that woman so bad I couldn't even keep anything on my stomach."[18] Using the pretext of the restaurant's sign being destroyed by a windstorm (a metaphor of the damage about to be caused by Frank's and Cora's sexual relationship), Frank convinces Nick to leave and get a replacement in Los Angeles, some twenty miles away. Finally having his chance with Nick gone, Frank attacks Cora, violently seducing her. But their lovemaking is not gentle or tender. It is conceived in violence, motivated by violence, and results in further violence. As Frank takes Cora in his arms and "mashes" his mouth against hers, she says: " 'Bite me! Bite me!' ":

> I bit her. I sunk my teeth into her lips so deep I could feel the blood spurt into my mouth. It was running down her neck when I carried her upstairs.[19]

Frank's sexual "capture" of Cora ironically turns against him as Cora's power (the power of the dark angel) takes hold of him, causing him to be twisted by her demands, forcing him to relinquish his single valuable possession—freedom. Cain establishes a nice descriptive contrast for Cora which helps to reveal her dangerous nature. Nick thinks of Cora as his "white dove," a beautiful, peaceful creature symbolic of love (which the reader quickly sees is false). Frank, on the other hand, sees Cora as a snarling cougar (he "liked her that way"), a predatory, meat-eater who is anything but loving. Cora connives with Frank into entering a murderous conspiracy to kill her husband. Frank agrees, and the trap of Fate is set.

Their first attempt would have worked if Fate, in the guise of a state policeman, hadn't interfered. Cora and Frank plan to have Nick killed in his bathtub, making it look like an accident. But a policeman arrives as Frank is standing guard under the bathroom window with a ladder. Before Frank can warn Cora, a cat unexpectedly climbs the ladder, steps on the electrical fuse box, shorting it out. The place is thrown into darkness; Cora strikes Nick and screams. The policeman and Frank respond, and Cora claims Nick slipped and hit his head when the lights went out. Nick is not killed, but is instead rushed to the hospital. Fate's demolition of Frank and of Cora herself is not immediate. It builds in scope through the story as the dark angel and her consort, at first warned of the consequences of their criminal intentions, do not curb their lust and violence. And even though Frank recognizes what a "bad" turn of Fate can do to them, he remains under Cora's domination:

Even if we had gone through with it they would have guessed it. They *always* guess it. They guess it anyway, just from habit. Because look how quick that cop knew something was wrong. That's what makes my blood run cold. Soon as he saw me standing there he knew it. If he could tumble to it all that easy, how much chance would we have if the Greek had died?[20]

Nick returns from the hospital and Frank leaves Cora, trying on unsuccessfullly to earn enough money at "pool-sharking" to financially entice her away from the restaurant. Fate intervenes again, and Nick meets Frank in Glendale, California, inviting him back to the restaurant and his old job. Upon returning, Frank is told by Cora that Nick wants her to have a child:

"I can't have no greasy Greek child, Frank. I can't, that's all. The only one I can have a child by is you. I wish you were some good. You're smart, but you're no good."[21]

Cora, the dark angel, can be the mother of no human child, only death. But part of her evil power, in addition to her sexual manipulation, is her guile. She knows that Frank is not smart, yet she tells him that he is to build up his ego. She promises him a child if he follows her will; by saying that he is no "good," a double meaning is suggested. The obvious implication is that he is an immoral individual; however, Cora twists the meaning so that it implies that Frank is no "good" as a killer. Cora thus motivates Frank to try again.

This time Frank plans "such a lousy murder it wouldn't even be a murder." Cora and Frank take Nick on a car trip to "the worst piece of road in Los Angeles County," there to kill him and make it look like an auto accident produced by too much drinking. Frank clubs Nick over the head. To make the accident seem realistic, he pours wine over the corpse and tips the car over the edge of the road. Then, he hits Cora in the eye, giving her a bruise that would appear to have been caused by the crash:

I hauled off and hit her in the eye as hard as I could. She went down. She was right down there at my feet, her eyes shining, her breasts trembling, drawn up in tight points, and pointing right up at me. She was down there, and the breath was roaring in the back of my throat like I was some kind of an animal, and my tongue was all swelled up in my mouth, and blood pounding in it.[22]

Next to the corpse of her dead husband, Cora makes love to Frank, a supreme act of sexual degradation. Frank has indeed become some kind of animal, an animal like Cora, stripped of his senses and encouraged to give free reign to his base animal instincts of lust and violence. He has reached a point of no return, has ignored the warnings of Fate, and now must pay the social price, forfeiting what little personal freedom he has left (after what Cora has taken) to the system.

Frank turns the car over on himself after the culmination of his lust with Cora is completed (again to make the crash look real), and is taken to the hospital with Cora and Nick's corpse. While at the hospital, District Attorney Sackett tricks Frank into signing a criminal complaint against Cora by telling him that he knew that they killed Frank. Angered by this act, Cora testifies against Frank, describing in detail their murder plans. Frank acquires the aid of a crafty attorney named Katz, and despite the weight of the evidence against them, he gets Frank and Cora off the murder charge by working the insurance companies (who held accident policies on Nick) against each other. Katz does this not because he is convinced of Frank's and Cora's innocence, but because of a bet made with Sackett. Cain thus illustrates that law in society can be reduced to a wager (another type of sparring match for personal ego instead of a forum of justice), and that guilt can be forgotten for monetary gain.

Frank and Cora get back together after their acquittal, despite the fact that they betrayed each other's love and trust. It is easy for them to flame that love, since the foundation of their relationship is constructed from animal desire, as shown by Cain in their sexual reunion:

"Rip me, Frank, Rip me like you did that night." I ripped all her clothes off. She twisted and turned, slow, so they would slip out from under her. Then she closed her eyes and lay back on the pillow. Her hair was falling over her shoulders in snaky curls. Her eye was all black, and her breasts weren't drawn up and pointing up at me, but soft and spread out in two big pink splotches. She looked like the great grandmother of every whore in the world. The devil got his money's worth that night.[23]

Cora, the hell-cat, the sex-snake (who "twists" and "turns" Frank's will to her own with her lovemaking) once more has Frank's soul. He remains with her a while at the restaurant, and starts to have another affair with a woman. But Cora quickly ends that, by being temporarily insane and they marry. Fate, like the postman of the novel's title, always "rings" twice, and visits a final conclusive catastrophe upon them. Cora is pregnant by Frank, and as he rushes her to the hospital because of a severe pain she is having, he has an accident on the road, killing Cora. This time, the wily Katz is unable to save Frank:

Katz fought them with every law book in Los Angeles County, but the judge let it in all about us murdering the Greek. Sackett said that fixed me up with a motive. That and just being a mad dog. Katz never even let me take the stand. What could I say? That I didn't do it, because we had just fixed it up, all the trouble we had had over killing the Greek? That would have been swell. The jury was out five minutes. The judge said he would give me exactly the same consideration he would show any other mad dog.[24]

Cora's last act for Frank is to put him in the electric chair. His new bride is death, the marriage performed by Fate.

The Postman Always Rings Twice presents a sociological comment on two issues: 1) the motif complex of the dark angel as an examination of the relationship between "good" sex and "bad" sex, and 2) the motif complex of urban alienation as a larger statement of the Great Depression in America.

In society, sexuality, marriage and the family are maintained by social control.[25] The fiction noir dark angel, however, as betokening "bad" sex (that is motivated by lust and violence), highlights the consequences of that violation of religious control. The result of Frank's and Cora's promiscuous transgressions, the product of their "love," is murder (and self-destruction). In Cain's novel and other fiction noir stories featuring the dark angel, the world where animal desire controls the actions of the protagonists becomes a world where those protagonists are ravaged by animal forces. The formula thus serves to explicate the dangers of "bad" sex, and advocate compliance to religious controls. Frank and Cora not only are doomed by their actions, their bloodline immortality is destroyed as well. Similar to supernatural sub-formulas, like the Gothic, Fate is used in the fiction noir formula as a power beyond human control that enters into the mortal sphere when religious control is disregarded (when "bad" sex is nurtured) to confound and destroy the transgressors. Unlike the supernatural formula, however, Fate is not embodied as a supernatural motif complex but instead as a hostile expression of the power of urban alienation: the governmental system.

It is no mere coincidence that the fiction noir formula began in the midst of America's Great Depression. Government and the trappings of government (i.e. laws, police, bureaucratic legislators, etc.) must continually act to reinforce their validity to members of society. They must be durable like the gods themselves.[26] The failure of the American government as perceived by the people (and it *is* perception that counts sociologically; it can be debated whether the government *actually* forsakened its constituents by allowing the Depression to happen or by neglecting the misery of the unemployed during this period) was taken as a "sign" of divine disfavor, not as an indication of any failure of the system itself. The "gods" were unhappy with the moral and economic excesses of the 1920s, and so the American people saw the Depression as a moral consequence, rather than a political one. If seen as a political problem, the people would have changed the system (adopting, say, a Marxist form of government), which they did not do. Instead they internalized the social problems of unemployment, structuring, in part, those problems in the fiction noir formula with the dark angel motif complex, a literary articulation of what "bad" things happen to those characters who repeat the moral excesses of the 1920s. Fate and the system, as divine forces, destroy the offenders before they can infect the morals of the larger society. The evil lies not with Fate or the system but with the individual. Urban alienation is thus explained as the threat to the validity of the institution by aberrant individuals:[27] the deviant is alienated so that the system can continue and the system must continue since it is legislated by the "gods."

Notes

[1]Robert Sampson, *Yesterday's Faces, Volume I: Glory Figures,* (Bowling Green, Oh.: Green University Popular Press, 1983), p. 15.

[2]Francis M. Nevins, Jr., "Cornell Woolrich," *Twentieth-Century Crime and Mystery Writers,* John M. Reilly, ed., (New York: St. Martin's Press, 1980), p. 511.

[3]Francis M. Nevins, Jr., "Introduction," *The Bride Wore Black* Cornell Woolrich (New York: Ballantine, 1984), pp. vii-x.

[4]Cornell Woolrich, "Angel Face," *The Great American Detective* William Kittredge

and Steven M. Krauzer, eds. (New York: Mentor Books, 1978), p. 233.

⁵*Ibid.*, pp. 232-233.

⁶*Ibid.*, p. 233.

⁷Peter L. Berger and Thomas Luckmann, *The Social Construction of Reality* (Garden City: Doubleday, 1966), p. 49.

⁸Woolrich, pp. 235-236.

⁹*Ibid.*, p. 239.

¹⁰Peter L. Berger, *The Sacred Canopy: Elements of a Sociological Theory of Religion* (Garden City: Doubleday, 1967), p. 85.

¹¹*Ibid.*, p. 85.

¹²John S. Whitley, "James M. Cain," *Twentieth-Century Crime and Mystery Writers*, John M. Reilly, ed., (New York: St. Martin's Press, 1980), p. 246.

¹³*Ibid.*, p. 247.

¹⁴*Ibid.*

¹⁵James M. Cain, *The Postman Always Rings Twice* (New York: Grosset & Dunlap, 1934), pp. 89-90.

¹⁶*Ibid.*, p. 6.

¹⁷*Ibid.*, p. 9.

¹⁸*Ibid.*, pp. 12-13.

¹⁹*Ibid.*, p. 15.

²⁰*Ibid.*, p. 39.

²¹*Ibid.*, p. 59.

²²*Ibid.*, pp. 71-72.

²³*Ibid.*, pp. 138-139.

²⁴*Ibid.*, p. 185.

²⁵Berger, p. 39.

²⁶*Ibid.*, p. 36.

²⁷*Ibid.*, pp. 36-37.

CHAPTER V
Gangster Formula

The Betrayal of the Trust:
The Bad Gangster and the Good Gangster

THE PASSAGE OF THE 18TH amendment to the United States Constitution in 1919 (the Prohibition Amendment: making it illegal to manufacture, sell or transport alcoholic spirits within the boundaries of the U.S.) gave a "face-lift" to organized crime, in effect, paradigmatically re-structuring the operations of criminals into a powerful social force. Prior to the enforcement of the Prohibition Amendment, crime was primarily unorganized: "The ordinary murderer, highwayman, thief, or embezzler is an unorganized criminal who operates by himself. When he commits a crime the hand of everyone in society is raised against him. He is easily apprehended, speedily convicted, and lands in the penitentiary with little difficulty."[1] After the enactment of Prohibition, however, crime radically altered, becoming organized so that greater profits could be made by "bootlegging" liquor and so that greater protection could be gained against the government(s): "The other class of criminals, the organized groups, work in gangs running from two to three to almost any number. They may devote their energies to one community, or spread across the country from coast to coast, or become international in their scope. Among these are racketeers of all kinds—kidnappers, bank-robbers, bootleggers, dope-peddlers, and confidence men."[2] Paradoxically, when the 18th Amendment was approved, it was believed by the supporters of Prohibition that the law could be enforced (after all, Section 2 of the Amendment empowered local, state and federal governments with the authority to arrest violators). In his book *Prohibition Legal and Illegal* (1928), Howard Lee McBain states: "The eighteenth amendment is aimed at individuals and the only way that individual conduct can be controlled is by prescribing punishments, detecting violations and instituting prosecutions."[3] What happened in

77

actuality was that the law covered an area of human conduct that could not be uniformly enforced. And as crime became more effectively organized in the manufacture, distribution and protection of alcohol, government agencies, like the police and court systems, were proved to be at best ineffective, and at worst, corrupt (as the gangsters discovered how easy it was to shield their operations by bribing the "right" people). No other legal act in American history so damaged the system meant to be protected, and by the time the 21st Amendment, the repeal of Prohibition, was passed in 1933, the destruction was done. Crime, powerful organized crime, was here to stay.

The advent of organized crime in American society was well documented by the mass media. Newspaper accounts of gang wars and mob slayings were "front-page" news in the 1920s and 1930s. Criminal activity became defined as a socially threatening situation where strong sanctions were required to reinforce the social norm.[4] Social reaction came in two forms. First, for those members of the culture where organized crime was perceived as "evil," society motivated its legal gatekeepers to seek and destroy criminal activity, to exercise the use of "official" violence (symbolizing that violence in religious terms).[5] In entertainment mass media of this period, the gangster was a figure every bit as prominent as he was in the news. And thus was nurtured the bad gangster sub-formula. Movies like *Little Caesar, Scarface* and *Public Enemy* (based in part on the lives of real criminals), for example, were extremely popular with film audiences since they depicted the violent destruction of evil, deviant mob leaders (hence, through violence, cleaning society of its social cancer). In the action/adventure comic strips, like *Dick Tracy*, gangsters were physical representations of actual crime figures exaggerated to grotesque proportions and contrasted with clean-cut, square-jawed heroes who gave them their "just desserts."[6] The pulp magazines contributed their fair share, as titles were created, such as *The Feds, Ace G-Man, Public Enemy* and *G-Man Detective*, which fictionally recounted J. Edgar Hoover's war on organized crime (with ritualistic success) in the 1930s. Second, for those members of society where organized crime was perceived as "good," as a sympathetic micro-system that battled the macro-system of corruption (laws, governments, etc.), the gangster was seen as a type of hero.

As migrant groups of unskilled workers immigrated to America from Europe just before and after the turn of the twentieth century in search of a "land of opportunity," they quickly discovered the harsh realities of that phrase. They encountered poor working conditions in their new home, and found little support from the local and state governments. In addition, they were met with prejudicial hostility from the larger society, and were ridiculed, taken advantage of as they became "fodder" for the growing industrial machines of the Gilded Age. The immigrant's sole avenue for survival lay in the security of numbers. They formed ghetto ethnic communities in the major East Coast and Mid-West cities, and within their own social worlds they developed methods of protection against the larger, malevolent world. Gangs formed within these ghettoes, and though the leaders of the gangs were defined as evil by the system (since they tended to prey on society), the immigrants themselves saw the gangster heads as rebel heroes. And as criminals like Al Capone received more and more media attention, middle-class America began to admire the gangster as courageous, compelling fortune-hunters. American historian Daniel J. Boorstin notes: "The remarkable rise of organized crime in the twentieth century is only another episode in the saga of restless new Americans reaching for opportunities to enlarge their fortunes and to rise in the world."[7] "American gangsters," Boorstin continues, "who only recently had arrived as down-trodden peasants, became rich businessmen and mayor-makers. And these quickly took their place in the iridescent American folklore of adventuring Go-Getters."[8] The good gangster sub-formula subsequently evolved in popular fiction, and evidenced this "Go-Getter" spirit that Boorstin describes, as we shall see later in Mario Puzo's novel *The Godfather*.

One of those pulp writers who successfully traced the literary growth of the bad gangster sub-formula between the 18th and 21st Amendments was Canadian/American author Frank L. Packard (1877-1942). His novel *The Big Shot* illustrates the encasement of the bad gangster motif complex of the betrayal of trust within the sub-formula.

Packard began writing for popular magazines in 1906, initially drawing upon his experience as an employee of the Canadian Pacific Railroad, and he published his first book in 1911, an anthology of railroad adventure fiction entitled *On the Iron at Big Cloud*. That first book, plus two later publications, *The Night Operator* (1919) and *Running Special* (1925), ranked Packard as one "of only two living writers [in 1940, that was] of the Railroad school" according to Frank P. Donavan, Jr., in his study *The Railroad in Literature*. But Packard was a writer of many talents, and he strove to work in a number of sub-formulas of the mystery genre (besides railroad adventure fiction).

1911 to 1917 were productive years for Packard. Not only did he publish one short story collection and six novels, he formulated three of the four literary subject areas that he was to later find great success in for years to come. In addition to his railroad fiction, *The Adventures of Jimmy Dale* (1917) and *The Further Adventures of Jimmy Dale* (1917) blazed a new path in pulp (and popular) fiction, creating and refining the bad gangster sub-formula. He was a successful author of romance fiction as well, aptly demonstrated by his novels *Greater Love Hath No Man* (1913) and *The Beloved Traitor* (1915). Packard's fourth type of story, the South Sea crime adventure, did not appear until a number of years later.

Before taking a look at *The Big Shot,* a review of two Packard themes that persist in nearly all of his fiction is in order, the first being that appearances are deceiving and the second that the untangling of appearances can result in success or destruction for the hero (or heroine). For Packard, the "howdunit" is secondary to the "whodunit." His stories depart from typical classical detective fiction of the mystery genre in that they present their crimes and the perpetrators of these crimes early on in the plot's action. In most classical detective fiction (as we shall see in Chapter Eight), the reader is presented with a crime puzzle. The detective hero pieces the clues to the puzzle and consequently discovers how the crime was committed and who committed it. Needless to say, this type of mystery genre sub-formula features aristocratic detectives solving crimes in aristocratic settings. Classical detective fiction can be considered "boring" (in comparison to the gangster formula) since essentialy its plot is retroactive and lacking in physical action.

In Packard's bad gangster crime fiction, the energy of the plot revolves around the villain's identity and the hero's ability to unmask the scoundrel before he can do any more damage to society. Knowledge of how the various crimes are executed is quickly outlined and dispensed with so that the reader can get to the "meat" of the story, which for Packard (and for many of the detective formula dime novels that he no doubt drew upon for inspiration, and for the "character," or hero, pulp wordsmiths of the 1930s who subsequently imitated Packard) was the hero's cleverness in revealing deception. Thus, in typical Packard fashion, the heroes of his novels are innocent men or women, wrongly accused, who strive to clear their good names (i.e., Jimmie Dale in the Gray Seal stories). The antagonists in these conflicts are bad gangster figures who stand to profit in some way by the hero's failure.

Packard invites the reader to be "tricked" by appearance, the appearance of the crime, the appearance of the bad gangster and the appearance of the hero. And as these appearances are pulled out of Packard's literary magic hat, we the reader, as much as the protagonist, sort truth from falsehood, fact from fiction. Often, Packard's heroes operate in disguise so that they can be more effective as society's moral champions against the underworld. Their disguises are crucial in their quest for success.

Disguise, truthful vision and moral ambiguity all serve as significant themes in *The Big Shot*, and it is quite fitting that the action of the story begins in an Italian, New York East Side diner, the Gondola Restaurant. "It did a thriving business," Packard describes. "It smiled alike on the just and on the unjust; and since its clientele was admittedly composed of more than a mere sprinkling of the latter, the Gondola had an air about it—as though something were always just going to happen." Things do indeed happen. Enid Howard, the heroine of the novel, meets Phil Martin, a reporter for the *Herald Star*, at the Gondola where he informs her that he is "hot on the trail" of a "super-gangster," known to members of the underworld and the police as the Big Shot. Martin is after a photograph of the mob leader, the only one known to exist, to publish in his paper.

Martin's underworld contact for the photo is Shive Frank. Afraid for his life, afraid to get near Martin, Frank trails Enid Howard and finally slips her the photograph. Before her eyes, Frank is gunned down by the Big Shot's gangsters. As she escapes from the scene of the execution, she examines the photo and discovers that the picture is of her brother, Roy, reported missing in World War I. Her quest begins, then, to learn the true identity of Big Shot.

Enid Howard thus makes a moral decision that is crucial for the Packard protagonist, a choice to disguise herself and descend into the underworld to track down the Big Shot. To find the truth, Enid disguises herself as a crook and has to act like a crook, which jeopardizes her mortal soul. Her odyssey takes her to the "slime and backwaters" of the dark city. Such a descent leads to suffering (as it does to the light angel in the fiction noir formula), especially when Phil Martin thinks that Enid is collaborating with the Big Shot. The gangster captures Enid and Martin together and proves that he is not Enid's brother (by showing them a defect in his foot: and symbolically, in his moral fiber) demonstrating that he is in reality the Big Shot, "Norry" Kane. Enraged at being betrayed by Enid (for he had romantic intentions for her), he plans to kill them. Martin realizes his mistake in condemning Enid, and with the specter of death a witness, he renews his love for her.

Enid and Phil escape the wrath of Norry Kane, but Kane himself cannot escape his own violent destiny. Locked in mortal combat with a rival gang, Kane is killed. Lovers are re-born through the death of evil. Kane is defined as a bad gangster because he seeks to further his own gains in social power at the expense of others, and because of his animal-like lust for Enid. He possesses no redeeming virtues that would make him a rebel hero to the socially oppressed. Thus, Packard's use of the motif complex of the betrayal of trust, of Kane's trust of Enid's criminal nature, functions to eliminate evil, Kane's evil, and restore society via Phil's "healthy" love for Enid.

Mario Puzo, with his good gangster novel *The Godfather* (1969), utilizes the betrayal of trust motif complex in a significantly different way. Puzo (1920-) worked a short stint as a messenger for the New York Central Railroad, and after World War II as a public relations administrator for the United States Air Force in Europe. During the 1960s he was an editor of *Male* magazine, later finally becoming a free-lance novelist and book-reviewer. Several of his novels published during this period include *The Dark Arena* (1955), *The Fortunate Pilgrim* (1965) and *The Runaway Summer of Davie Shaw (1966)*. But with the release of *The Godfather*, Puzo catapulted his literary career into bestseller status, receiving close to $500,000 in advance money for hardcover, paperback and movie rights.[9] By 1970, *The Godfather* laid claim to the largest first-printing in the history of paperback books, while the movie adapted from the novel was financially and critically very successful, receiving three Academy Awards (the sequel movie, *The Godfather: Part II* also received three Oscars).[10]

In looking at the opening frame device of the novel, the wedding of Don Vito Corleone's daughter, Puzo elaborates on: 1) the power of Corleone's "family" to institute a type of social justice for the people under Corleone's (the Godfather's) protection, and 2) the consequences for breaking "faith" with Corleone's "trust."

As the story opens, Sicilian immigrant Amerigo Bonasera has just seen the release (by the U.S. Courts) of two young men who tried to rape his daughter and he makes a decision:

All his years in America, Amerigo Bonasera had trusted in law and order. And he had prospered thereby. Now, though his brain smoked with hatred, though wild visions of buying a gun and killing the two young men jangled the very bones of his skull, Bonasera turned to his still uncomprehending wife and explained to her, "They have made fools of us." He paused and then made his decision, no longer fearing the cost. "For justice we must go on our knees to Don Corleone."[11]

For Bonasera, when the courts fail to execute "justice" and set free the "animales" who should have been punished, Puzo has defined an American society where the laws work against the immigrant, and where the only force to enact justice is wielded by the head of a criminal mob. Thus, the mob is portrayed as a more effective and equitable organization than the government. When Bonasera talks to Don Corleone at the wedding, the Godfather replies that his feelings are wounded, but that he " 'is not that sort of person who trusts friendship on those who do not value it—or those who think him of little account.' "[12] Vito Corleone promises to give Bonasera his justice (by beating up the men who hurt Bonasera's daughter) only if Bonasera in turn promises his "friendship" to Corleone, that plus a promise to return the "favor" sometime in the future. This scene illustrates the structure of the Godfather's domination of others, a domination based on reciprocal trust and reciprocal obligation. The breaking of that trust, as we shall note later, is a direct threat not only to the Don's effective authority, but to the power of the Don's organization to help others as well.

When his Godson, Johnny Fontane, approaches the Don at the wedding for a favor (to get a part in a new movie that will elevate his career as an entertainer), Corleone replies: " 'Friendship is everything. Friendship is more than talent. It is more than government. It is almost the equal of family. Never forget that. It you had built up a wall of friendships you wouldn't have to ask me to help.' "[13] Needless to say, Godfather Corleone lands Johnny the movie role (by threatening violence against the "hard-headed" film producer who hates Johnny). A conversation between Michael, Don Vito's youngest son, and his girlfriend Kay during the wedding informs the reader of the Godfather's meaning of the phrase "wall of friendship":

Kay said thoughtfully, "Are you sure you're not jealous of your father? Everything you've told me about him shows him doing something for other people. He must be good-hearted." She smiled wryly. "Of course his methods are not exactly constitutional."
Michael sighed, "I guess that's the way it sounds, but let me tell you this. You know those Arctic explorers who leave caches of food scattered on route to the North Pole? Just in case they may need them someday? That's my father's favors. Someday he'll be at each one of those people's houses and they had better come across."[14]

The plot of Puzo's *The Godfather*, though detailing the myriad facets of the Don's influence on the lives of a number of people, specifically narrates the transition of power from the "old" order (Vito Corleone) to the "new" (Vito's son, Michael). At the age of twelve, Vito had escaped to America from the Sicilian Mafia. The Mafia had killed his father in a dispute there and feared that the son might seek revenge. Once in New York, Vito tries to make an honest living, but soon learns that the honest immigrants are easy prey for criminals and an uncaring government. Deciding to organize a mob, Corleone fast rises to authority in the ghetto, and as the following paragraph demonstrates, this Algerian social ascent favorably benefits those who hang on his coattails:

The Great Depression increased the power of Vito Corleone. And indeed it was about that time that he came to be called Don Corleone. Everywhere in the city, honest men begged for honest work in vain. Proud men demeaned themselves and their families to accept official charity from a contemptuous officialdom. But the men of Don Corleone walked the streets with their heads held high, their pockets stuffed with silver and paper money. With no fear of losing their jobs. And even Don Corleone, that most modest of men, could not help feeling a sense of pride. He was taking care of his world, his people. He had not failed those who depended on him and gave him the sweat of their brows, risked their freedom and their lives in his service.[15]

Puzo thus describes the superiority of the Corleone system of social justice (and protection) over that of the government. But the "catch" to this ghetto utopia is unwavering loyalty to the leader. "This of course was not pure Christian charity," Puzo continued. "Not his best friends would have called Don Corleone a saint from heaven. There was some self-interest in this generosity."[16] Vito Corleone—as a literal "God"-"father" in that his will has an omnipotent, yet fatherly flavor—is symbolized as the benefactor institution of law and morality superior to that of the larger society. He represents divine justice and divine sympathy who patterns the conduct of those around him into structures of acceptable conduct. The positive outcome of his methods suggests a kind of legitimation where significant others are socialized to incorporate honor, trust and justice into their collective identities. The betrayal of the Godfather's legitimizing authority documents a chaotic attack against positive social order.

Michael's transition into the Godfather's role demonstrates his evolving dedication to the superior gangster social order, and he is motivated by his witnessing the destructive outcomes resulting from various individuals' betrayal of trust of the Godfather's disciplined moral vision. Michael, at the beginning of the story, is an "outsider" to the family business by choice. He disobeys his father's wishes by enlisting in the army during World War II, by dating a non-Sicilian girl, and by desiring to lead his own life as he sees fit. However, circumstances change that attitude. Vito Corleone is "set up" for a "hit" when he refuses to become part of a drug-dealing operation that the other families want to establish in America. The person who set up Vito, a gangster named Paulie Gatto (the Don's bodyguard), is appropriately dealt with for his betrayal:

For Clemenza [a captain of the Godfather's family] planned to handle this job himself, not only to help a new inexperienced man make his bones, but to settle a personal score with Paulie Gatto. Paulie had been his protege, he had advanced Paulie over the heads of more deserving and more loyal people, he had helped Paulie "make his bones" and furthered his career in every way. Paulie had not only betrayed the Family, he had betrayed his *padrone*, Peter Clemenza. This lack of respect had to be repaid.[17]

Michael saves his father's life when agents of the rival families, discovering that the Don was not killed by their first attempt, try again in the hospital where Vito is recovering. Michael gets injured for his efforts (his jaw is broken by a corrupt police captain when he sees Michael guarding the hospital). Later, when a meeting is arranged to try and make peace using Michael as the "go-between," Michael abandons his neutrality towards family business and desires to be the "button-man" (or executioner) of those gangsters who attacked his father, who betrayed the trust of his father and who betrayed the peace among the rival families. As Michael tells his father's "councilor" Tom Hagan:

"Tom, don't let anybody kid you. It's all personal, every bit of business. Every piece of shit every man has to eat every day of his life is personal. They call it business. OK. But it's personal as hell. You know where I learned that from? The Don. My old man. The Godfather. If a bolt of lightning hit a friend of his the old man would take it personal. That's what makes him great. The Great Don. He takes everything personal. Like God...."[18]

Michael thus kills the men who tried to kill his father, finally taking his place as an "inside" member of the family. And as the plot reaches its conclusion, with Michael as the new Don, the new Godfather, working his family the same way his father had, he has achieved his destiny in life. All the major and minor episodes of *The Godfather* revolve around the betrayal of trust motif complex (as first developed by Packard). The novel is a "shaggy-dog" story of connected events where the identities of family betrayers are detected and dealt with, according to the family's code of honor. As a threat to the stability of the social institution (the Godfather's family), the betrayal of trust is countered by incisive, violent methods since the destruction of that institution advocates irrationality.

The appeal of the good gangster sub-formula for its audience is twofold. On the one hand, the simplicity of the Godfather's methods in dealing with social problems is attractive since that simplicity (and effectiveness) eliminates the "red-tape" otherwise encountered by "going by" the system. In addition, the moral products of the Godfather's methods prove of substantial benefit for those who are helpless in the face of larger social evils (perpetuated by the very system that the Godfather himself counter-manipulates). On the other hand, *The Godfather* is a story of a "family" that offers survival for its members.[19] Michael's reunion with his family symbolizes not only his faith in the family's governing abilty to protect his (and significant other's) survival, it suggests a method by which one can find success (both financial and emotional) in life, and control over otherwise hostile forces.

Notes

[1]Philip S. Van Cise, *Fighting the Underworld* (Boston: Houghton Mifflin, 1936), p. 3.
[2]*Ibid.*, p. 3.
[3]Howard Lee McBain, *Prohibition Legal and Illegal* (New York: Macmillan, 1928), p. 21.
[4]Peter L. Berger, *The Sacred Canopy: Elements of a Sociological Theory of Religion* (Garden City: Doubleday, 1967), p. 44.
[5]*Ibid.*, p. 44.
[6]Garyn G. Roberts, "The Many Faces of Dick Tracy." (Bowling Green: unpublished Thesis, Bowling Green State University, 1983), pp. 55-66.
[7]Daniel J. Boorstin, *The Americans: The Democratic Experience* (New York: Random House, 1973), p. 84.
[8]*Ibid.*, p. 86.
[9]Jane A. Bowden, ed., *Contemporary Authors, Volumes 65-68* (Detroit: Gale Research Co., 1977), p. 474.
[10]*Ibid.*, p. 474.
[11]Mario Puzo, *The Godfather* (New York: Putnam's, 1969), p. 10.
[12]*Ibid.*, p. 29.
[13]*Ibid.*, p. 36.
[14]*Ibid.*, p. 41.
[15]*Ibid.*, p. 213.
[16]*Ibid.*
[17]*Ibid.*, p. 100.
[18]*Ibid.*, p. 145.
[19]Berger, p. 133.

CHAPTER VI
Thief Formula

E.W. Hornung's Amateur Cracksman: The Rise of the Bad Thief

MOVING CLOSER TO THE RATIONAL end of the mystery genre spectrum, next to the gangster formula on the left hand and to the thriller formula on the right, is the thief formula. The origins of the thief formula of the mystery genre began in a series of twelve interconnected short stories featuring the master crook, Colonel Clay, written by the English author Grant Allen and appearing in *The Strand Magazine* from June 1896 through May 1897. These stories were later collected in the book *An African Millionaire* (1897).[1]

Colonel Clay, in addition to being a master crook, was a master of disguise, and he could alter his face and manners at will, fooling everyone around him. The single victim of Clay's attacks was Sir Charles Vandrift, the African diamond millionaire, an obtuse man housing the character faults of greed and stupidity, which, of course, left him at the mercy of the devious Clay. Each short story recounted a new scheme of Clay's to relieve Vandrift of some of his great wealth, using disguise and Vandrift's own greedy ambition to his successful advantage. In effect, Clay was a robber stealing from another "robber baron" figure, stealing from one who steals from others. But, technically speaking, since Vandrift was the central protagonist of each story and not Clay, Allen's crook was not the first thief to function as the "hero" (or anti-hero) of the formula. That distinction belongs to E.W. Hornung's gentleman burglar and amateur cracksman, A.J. Raffles.

Ernest William Hornung (1866-1921) at age eighteen moved to Australia, remaining there for three years. Upon his return to England, his homeland, he married Constance Doyle (the sister, interestingly, of Sir Arthur Conan Doyle, who created another popular mystery hero of that era, Sherlock Holmes). Hornung was an expert on the game of cricket (a subject that was to figure significantly in his Raffles series), as well as being a respected player. Several of his fictional works dealt with his experience in Austrlia, including *The Rogue's March* (1896) and *Stingaree* (1905), while his later novels, such as *The Crime Doctor* (1914) and *Young Blood* (1898) dealt with the relationship between psychology and crime.[2] His Raffles stories, however, remain his best known and most popular work.

The first of Hornung's Raffles stories started appearing in England around 1889, and from then until 1909, three anthologies, *The Amateur Cracksman* (1899), *Raffles* (1901) and *A Thief In the Night* (1905), and one novel, *Mr. Justice Raffles* (1909), were published.[3] The Raffles character was revived after Hornung's death by Philip Atkey (writing as Barry Perowne) and new short stories (set in a post-Victorian England) were featured in the British pulp magazine, *Thriller*, and the American pulp magazines *Thrilling Detective* and *Black Book Detective* through the 1930s.[4]

"The Ides of March," the opening story from Hornung's first Raffles collection, *The Amateur Cracksman*, introduces the reader to the suave Raffles, and to his accomplice in crime (his Watson to Doyle's Sherlock Holmes), "Bunny" Manders. As the tale begins, Bunny has just lost a large sum of money at the baccarat tables at the Hotel Albany. Bunny seeks his old friend, Raffles, in the hopes that he can be lent the money to cover his gambling debts. Raffles asks Bunny if his "people" (or family) can help him out, to which Bunny replies that he is an only child, that he has no people (for which Bunny is grateful since the knowledge of his misfortunes would shame him in their eyes). Bunny then notes Raffles' response to his plea:

... then, with a shrug, he resumed his walk, and for some minutes neither of us spoke. But in his handsome, unmoved face I read my fate and death-warrant; and with every breath I cursed my folly and my cowardice in coming to him at all. Because he had been kind to me at school, when he was captain of the eleven, and I his fag, I had dared to look for kindness from him now; because I was ruined, and he rich enough to play cricket all summer, and do nothing for the rest of the year, I had fatuously counted on his mercy, his sympathy, his help![5]

Bunny threatens to kill himself, but is held by Raffles' look: "Neither fear nor horror were in it; only wonder, admiration, and such a measure of pleased expectancy as caused me after all to pocket my revolver with an oath."[6]

Thus is the reader given a masterful insight into Raffles' character, a man who feels a thrill of excitement over violence (even if that violence concerns his friend) and who is impressed with fanatical dedication. Bunny surrenders his gun, and delivers a further insight about Raffles:

...Raffles had the subtle power of making himself irresistible at will. He was beyond comparison the most masterful man whom I have ever known; yet my acquiescence was due to more than the mere subjection of the weaker nature to the stronger.[7]

Raffles, as Bunny compares the man to himself, is a figure larger than life, a master of life and his own fate. He is one of the world's hunters (while Bunny is a victim) who, as we shall see, preys on those around him with skill ... and style.

Raffles reaffirms his friendship to Bunny, though he informs Bunny that he, too, is "hard up" for cash at the moment. As Raffles ponders what to do, Bunny himself contemplates Raffles' room, thinking him more the esthetic than the sportsman:

What struck me most, however, was the absence of the usual insignia of a cricketer's den. Instead of the conventional rack of war-worn bats, a carved oak bookcase, with every shelf in a litter, filled the better part of one wall; and where I looked for cricketing groups, I found reproductions of such works as "Love and Death" and "The Blessed Damozel," in dusty frames and different parallels. The man might have been a minor poet instead of an athlete of the first water.[8]

But Raffles indeed possesses a curious mixture of traits. He is an artist, an artist of crime, if you will, and an intellectual. In addition, he is an athlete of good "tone" (or style) who greets each episode of crime as a sports hero would greet an important game: with verve, dedication and fortitude. It is his attitude towards the "tone" of life that motivates him to enter a life of crime. Normally, crime is perceived by members of society as a product of social deviance. But the individual himself controls his own perception if a certain condition is met. If, for example, a person makes no contribution to the establishment of a socialization program, then he is more likely to deviate from it.[9] The rules of society are not Raffles' rules. Society dictates that stealing is wrong, and that hard work is good. Raffles dictates that stealing is right, if the results of stealing permit him to lead a life divorced from hard work (what the "lower" classes do for money) and permit him to pursue a fine style of living. Raffles' conceptualization of crime, then, serves as the foundation for the bad thief character who envisions crime as a method by which to improve one's life. Raffles is also defined as a bad thief because he steals for the thrill of it, as much as he does for survival. He sees the criminal act as a type of personal challenge in which the "style" of the theft is as important as the monetary reward. The bad thief is similar to the good gangster figure in that both believe the rules of society as endangering their existence, if they bend to those rules. If, however, they actively negotiate their own conduct as they see fit, if they become the hunter instead of the hunted, if they can manipulate those around them to their own will and if they collect those icons of wealth (take them from their "legal" owners) via deviant actions, then they survive. The difference, of course, between the bad thief and the good gangster is: 1) the gangster operates within a group, the bad thief as an individual, and 2) the good gangster seeks to improve the quality of life for a number of other people while the bad thief seeks only to improve his own.

Raffles asks Bunny if he " 'would stick at nothing for a pal,' "[10] even if that would entail planning a crime, to which Bunny replies: "No, not even at that ... name your crime, and I'm your man."[11] Bunny then escorts Raffles to a jewelry shop on Bond Street where Raffles uses his friend as a "look-out" while he robs the shop's safe. Bunny reluctantly cooperates, his moral sense making him feel a bit guilty, but they successfully complete the theft. Upon returning to the Albany, they divide the jewels (and Bunny now has the money to cover his gambling debts). Raffles makes Bunny the offer to remain his cohort in crime, to help him in future daring robberies, which places Bunny in a moral dilemma:

My blood froze. My heart sickened. My brain whirled. How I had liked this villain! How I had admired him! Now my liking and admiration must turn to loathing and disgust. I waited for the change. I longed to feel it in my heart. But—I longed and I waited in vain![12]

Bunny is forced into making a choice. He must decide whether he will abide by the rules of society or by Raffles' rules, and he must debate the values of both systems. Society has done very little in the way of promoting Bunny's welfare (it offered him no recourse but suicide, for example, with the non-payment of his gambling debts). Raffles' argument, on the other hand, is very convincing:

"...but I was in much the same fix that you were in tonight, and it [crime] was my only way out. I never meant it for anything more; but I'd tasted blood, and it was all over with me. Why should I work when I could steal? Why settle down to some humdrum uncongenial billet, when excitement, romance, danger and a decent living were all going begging together? Of course it's very wrong, but we can't all be moralists, and the distribution of wealth is very wrong to begin with."[13]

Bunny is swayed by Raffles' logic, and he finally takes an oath to be Raffles' man. Bunny recognizes, as does the reader, that personal survival takes precedence over social law, that life takes precedence over death; and the most famous partnership of crime in popular culture was ultimately consummated.

Hornung's bad thief sub-formula was to prove to be well-liked over the years, and imitated by a number of authors in both Europe and America. R. Austin Freeman (using the pen name Clifford Ashden) wrote a series of bad thief stories featuring Romney Pringle, most of which appeared in *Cassell's Magazine* and the *Windsor Magazine* between 1902 and 1903. These stories were collected in the books *Adventures of Romney Pringle* (1902) and *The Further Adventures of Romney Pringle* (1970),[14] and highlighted the lasting appeal of Freeman's Pringle over time. Maurice LeBlanc's Arsene Lupin was another important bad thief character to be contributed to the sub-formula. LeBlanc began publishing his Lupin series in France, and the stories were imported to the United States, released in the pulp, *The Popular Magazine*, and collected in the American edition, *The Exploits of Arsene Lupin* (1907). LeBlanc continued to sell Lupin stories and novels successfully until 1933.[15] The contemporary master of the mystery short story, Edward D. Hoch, released a number of very popular stories in *Ellery Queen's Mystery Magazine* during the 1960s, 1970s and 1980s detailing the exploits of Nick Velvet, again demonstrating that in a magazine dealing primarily with classical detective fiction, the bad thief story persistently encourages a strong following.

Thomas W. Hanshew's Man of Forty Faces: The Bad Thief Turns Good

Out of the mold of the bad thief story, Thomas W. Hanshew created the first modern good thief character, Hamilton Cleek. Like Raffles, the good thief at first recognizes the advantages of entering the business of crime for profit. Like the bad thief, he enjoys great prosperity, criminal triumph after criminal triumph, which insures personal survival. Unlike the bad thief, however, the good thief "backslides" from crime, reversing his contempt for society and society's rules and uses his skills to help the police and courts.

Hanshew (1857-1914) wrote hardcover novels for both the American and English markets around the turn of the nineteenth century. It is rumored by several detective fiction historians that Hanshew was a dime novelist, one of the many writers of the long-running Nick Carter series and an author who used the Berta M. Clay pseudonym.[16] J. Randolph Cox states that the reader who is unprepared or unable to suspend disbelief will never be able to read Hanshew, and that he is a "period author" who must be read in the context of his times and the tradition from which he came.[17] But Cox goes on to say that Hanshew did have an influence on contemporary mystery authors, like John Dickson Carr, who adopted Hanshew's method of creating ingenious situations and intricate plots.[18] Whatever the artistic merits of Hanshew, he enjoyed a great deal of popularity with his readers and published a number of bestselling mysteries, including the novels *Beautiful But Dangerous* (1891), *The World's Finger* (1901), *The Mallison Mystery* (1903), *The Great Ruby* (1905) *The Shadow of a Dead Man* (1906) and *Fate and the Man* (1910). In addition, he helped to shape a new direction for the thief formula which became widely copied by his peers.

As Hornung did, Hanshew sold his Cleek stories to the pulp magazines and hardcover publishers. A number of Cleek tales appeared in the American pulp *Short Stories* between 1913 and 1920, while the Cleek serial *The Riddle of the Night* was featured in *All-Story Weekly* in five parts from July 17 through August 14, 1915.[19] The common practice for pulp mystery writers during this period was first to release a series of loosely connected short stories then to gather those stories for book publication with each tale a chapter of the book. Hanshew did this with his Cleek material in *The Man of Forty Faces* (1910), *Cleek of Scotland Yard* (1914) and *Cleek's Greatest Riddles* (1916). Thus the author's work essentially earned two incomes, from the magazines and from the book publishers, making his efforts more profitable. It remains a custom for today's bestselling writers. The Cleek series was popular enough to warrant being pastiched, and the character was continued by Hanshew's wife and daughter a number of years after Hanshew's death.[20]

"The Affair of the Man Who Called Himself Hamilton Cleek" was the first short story to introduce the good thief character (appearing as the first chapter of *The Man of Forty Faces*) to the mystery genre. As the story opens, Constable Collins, on point duty at Blackfriar Bridge, is admiring a "French beauty" when he sees "a figure of a man in a gray frock-coat and a shining 'topper' " running down the street towards him. Hearing cries to head the man off and thinking him a pickpocket, Collins wrestles with the fleeing character. As he is grappling with the constable, the man tells Collins to make the struggle look good since they are being filmed for a " 'living picture, for the Alhambra tonight.' " Collins believes the story, and as a car pulls up to pick up the "actor" and the French woman, he is thrown a half-sovereign for his role. Collins then is derided by the onlooking crowd:

"Smart capture, Bobby, wasn't it?" sang out a . . . voice that set the crowd jeering . . . . "You'll git promoted, you will! See it in all the evenin' papers—oh, yus! 'Orrible hand-to-hand struggle with a desperado. Brave constable has 'arf a quid's worth out of an infuriated ruffian.' My hat! won't your missis be proud when you take her to see that bloomin' film?"[21]

Plainclothes detective Smathers finally shows up and demands of Collins why he did not stop the man. He chastises the constable for letting go the devil of "Forty Faces," the "Vanishing Cracksman," Hamilton Cleek and his confederate, "Margot, the Queen of the Apaches," and laments that they have lost two hundred quid in reward money. This scene illustrates the two motif complexes of the thief formula. First, it demonstrates the inefficiency and gullibility of the police, and it shows the contempt that the people have for the police. Second, it documents the skills of the thief as he confronts and tricks the system. It is indeed an unfair contest, as Collins regrets:

"Heavens!" gulped Collins, too far gone to say anything else, too deeply dejected to think of anything but that he had had the man for whom Scotland Yard had been groping for a year; the man over whom all England, all France, and all Germany wondered, close shut in the grip of his hands and then had let him go. He was the biggest and the boldest criminal the police had ever had to cope with, the almost supernatural genius of crime, who defied all systems, laughed at all laws, mocked at all the Vidocqs, and Lupins, and Sherlock Holmes, whether amateur or professional, French or English, German or American, that ever had or ever could be pitted against him, and who, for sheer devilry, for diabolical ingenuity, and for colossal impudence, as well as for a nature-bestowed power that was simply amazing, had not his match in all the universe.[22]

Cleek as the ultimate "trickster" is more than a match for Vidocq and Sherlock Holmes, two examples of that time of the best detective heroes, and his crimes are of international dimensions. The police of England, or of any nation, have little hope of catching him, killing him or reforming him since he possesses abilities far above their meager talents. He is a potent force for social evil, until a force greater than himself convinces him to reform: that being the love of a "good" woman.

After performing a daring theft, Cleek writes Scotland Yard saying that he plans to give up his criminal activities, and return some stolen jewelry as a token of his intent. During his interview with Superintendent Narkom and Sir Horace Wyvern of the Yard, Cleek informs them:

"That's why I have requested this interview. I want you to examine me, Sir

Horace, to put me through those tests you use to determine the state of mind of the mentally fit and mentally unfit. I want to know if it is my fault that I am what I am, and if it is myself I have to fight in the future or the devil that lives within me. I'm tired of wallowing in the mire. A woman's eyes have lit the way to heaven for me. I want to climb up to her, to win her, be worthy of her, and to stand beside her in the light."[23]

When told that he cannot be honest, cannot escape the devil, Cleek vows that he will " 'fight the devil with his own weapons and crush him under the weight of his own gifts.' "[24] On the Rational/Irrational spectrum of the mystery genre, Cleek is emblematic of the protagonist who *can* control his Fate, who *can* control the devil. The catalyst for that control comes from Ailsa Lorne, the beautiful and frail household manager of Sir Horace's, whom Cleek has fallen madly in love with. He discards his other female accomplice, Margot (the "evil" woman) who, out of spite turns against him to become one of his most savage antagonists in later stories. Lorne, beautiful, helpless, functions as the larger symbol of civilization. And since the laws of civilization are designed, in part, to protect the good woman and her off-spring (thus insuring rationality, stability and species' survival), Cleek dedicates himself to the protection of law (and the indirect protection of the good woman). Sociologically speaking, role reflects the relationship between society and the universe. In the good thief sub-formula, the good woman is a possible mother figure, and procreative activity with that woman symbolizes the procreation of the universe.[25] The good woman, as instrument of creation, becomes a bestower of immortality, while the bad woman represents the opposite, chaos and destruction (both moral and physical). Social law, serves as a formula for immortality in the good thief story. Social law transcends the political dictates of human action, and serves as a proscription of immortality in the good thief story. Without the good woman figure, the laws of society can, as in the bad thief sub-formula, be destructive to the individual (Raffles takes appropriate measures to insure his survival, which is the breaking of those laws). With the good woman figure (a motif complex in all good thief fiction) the good thief protagonist is motivated to change his nature, to become a servant of those laws, to become good, as Cleek states at the conclusion of the story:

"I've fought the law, now let me switch over and fight with it. I'm tired of being Cleek, the thief; Cleek, the burglar. Make me Cleek, the detective, and let us work together, hand in hand, for a common cause and for the public good."[26]

The good thief, however, *is* a thief figure because he, though helping the law, employs criminal methods. For example, to clear the reputation of a wrongly accused person, the good thief will rob a safe to acquire the needed evidence. To prevent a person from going to jail for robbery, the good thief will steal the money from someone who can afford the loss.

One of the next major mystery writers to work within the good thief sub-formula was Louis Joseph Vance. His eight books featuring Michael Lanyard the "Lone Wolf" were published from 1914 to 1934; his first Lanyard novel, *The Lone Wolf*, was initially released in *Munsey's Magazine* early in 1914.[27] But perhaps the most famous author to employ the good thief character was Frank L. Packard. His series of stories featuring Jimmie Dale, the Gray Seal, were collected in several volumes, including *The Adventures of Jimmie Dale* (1917) compiled from short stories published in the pulp *The People's Magazine* from 1914 through 1915, and *The Further Adventures of Jimmie Dale* (1919), gathered from *The People's Magazine*, 1916-1917. Packard wrote three Jimmie Dale novels, *Jimmie Dale and the Phantom Clue* (1922), *Jimmie Dale and the Blue Envelope Murder* (1930) and *Jimmie Dale and the Missing Hour* (1935).[28] As happens in the creation of popular fiction, the invention of a story by one author inspires another author to modify that story, involving a new sub-formula. Packard had that sort of impact upon the mystery genre, and his Gray Seal series helped form some motif complexes for the avenger detective sub-formula, which will be reviewed in Chapter Eight.

Notes

[1]Robert Sampson, *Yesterday's Faces, Volume I: Glory Figures* (Bowling Green: Bowling Green University Popular Press, 1983), p. 97.

[2]Chris Steinbrunner and Otto Penzler, eds., *Encyclopedia of Mystery & Detection* (New York: McGraw-Hill, 1976), p. 216.

[3]Sampson, p. 102.

[4]*Ibid.*

[5]E.W. Hornung, *The Amateur Cracksman* (New York: Scribner's, 1910), pp. 4-5.

[6]*Ibid.*, p. 6.

[7]*Ibid.*, p. 7.

[8]*Ibid.*, p. 11.

[9]Peter L. Berger and Thomas Luckman, *The Social Construction of Reality* (Garden City: Doubleday, 1966), p. 62.

[10]Hornung, p. 13.

[11]*Ibid.*

[12]*Ibid.*, p. 31.

[13]*Ibid.*, p. 33.

[14]Sampson, p. 107.

[15]*Ibid.*, p. 108.

[16]J. Randolph Cox, "Thomas W. Hanshew," *Twentieth-Century Crime and Mystery Writers*, John M. Reilly, ed., (New York: St. Martin's Press, 1980), p. 729.

[17]*Ibid.*

[18]*Ibid.*

[19]Sampson, p. 113.

[20]*Ibid.*, pp. 113-114.

[21]Thomas W. Hanshew, *Cleek—The Man of Forty Faces* (New York: McKinlay, Stone & Mackenzie, 1918), pp. 7-8.

[22]*Ibid.*, pp. 9-10.

[23]*Ibid.*, pp. 28-29.

[24]*Ibid.*, pp. 29-30.

[25]Peter L. Berger, *The Sacred Canopy: Elements of a Sociological Theory of Religion* (Garden City: Doubleday, 1967), p. 38.

[26]Hanshew, p. 30.

[27]Sampson, p. 121.

[28]*Ibid.*, p. 136.

CHAPTER VII
Thriller Formula

From American Dime Novel to British Bestseller:
The Evolution of the Charismatic Spy

THE MOST RATIONAL MYSTERY GENRE formula, aside from the detective formula, is the thriller (or spy) story. Here the spy hero begins to exert a positive influence on his environment (more so than does, say, the gangster or thief figure) by protecting or enforcing the rules of the dominant political system (as contrasted with the sub-culture mores of the gangster or the personal mores of the thief). Popular literature historian of the spy story, LeRoy L. Panek, states that "some isolated examples of spy literature appear early in the nineteenth century. We can ... trace the spy story back to one of Cooper's sillier novels, *The Spy* (1821), or to Poe's detective tale, 'The Purloined Letter,' (1845)."[1] Panek goes on to suggest that the above examples, though widely known in Britain and America, had little to do with the evolution of the spy story.[2] In locating those early tales which did significantly contribute to the structure of the thriller formula, two traditions are evidenced, one American and the other British, the former establishing the motif complexes of the charismatic spy sub-formula, the latter the motif complexes of the dark spy sub-formula; though, of course, over time these two sub-formulas crossed back and forth over the Atlantic so as to implant themselves as popular story forms of both countries.

The origins of the charismatic spy sub-formula appeared in American detective dime novels, specifically in the *New York Detective Library* (1882-1899) and *Secret Service* (1899-1912) with the character Old King Brady. Hoping to capitalize on the growing popularity of the "superhuman detective," dime novel publisher Frank Tousey decided to publish his own variant, Old King Brady, in the November 14, 1885 (number 154) issue of *New York Detective Library*. Tousey observed his sales figures with the first three years of this dime novel, and noted that the stories which featured a detective hero who was as physical as he was cerebral outsold those stories which featured the more traditional classical detective. In addition, Tousey witnessed the same growing tendency in competing dime novel detective fiction titles. With Brady's first "novel," we see a fictional universe where the detective hero is a superior individual. Old King Brady never failed to solve a mystery simply because he was an extraordinary man. He symbolized the rugged and durable American, parented by the robust frontiersman dime novel tradition. He was often called a sleuth (one of the earliest uses of the term), literally a "hound" of tremendous dependabilty and a creature of relentlessness. Most of the Brady stories (85 in the *Library*) were written by Francis Worcester Doughty, under the "house" penname of "A New York Detective." Doughty was known for his detailed and accurate settings. When he was unsure of a particular detail, he employed hundreds of maps and reference books to establish the correct setting or locale. In his first Brady story, Doughty detailed the New York City milieu with craft, from Broadway to lower Manhattan. That sense of the vast and dangerous city, most often thought to be the creation of the hard-boiled detective writers, was created by Doughty some 25 years before the first *Black Mask* "mean street." Little biographic information is known today about Doughty, as with so many of his dime novel peers, and hence the facts of his life exist in some overcrowded, forgotten dime novel "limbo."

As Brady left the confines of the *New York Detective Library*, transported to *Secret Service* by Tousey, an interesting transformation began. Brady's cases, which earlier had been rather straightforward examples of the classical sub-formula, started to become more political (and international) in scope. Brady was acting more like a spy, using "undercover" methods to root out other foreign and domestic spies. By the end of his tour of duty in *Secret Service*, Brady had established the two central motif complexes of the modern charismatic spy sub-formula: 1) the spy hero who operates in a world where "good" and "evil" are clearly defined (with the charismatic spy as agent of the "good" government); and 2) the spy hero who is smarter, braver, stronger and more sexually attractive—to a superhuman degree—than any other character in the story.

The first modern author to make use of the charismatic spy was bestselling novelist Ian Fleming (1908-1964). Most of Fleming's work dealt with his British Secret Service ace, James Bond, and over the course of the author's lifetime, twelve Bond novels: *Casino Royale* (1954), *Live and Let Die* (1954), *Moonraker* (1955), *Diamonds Are Forever* (1956), *From Russia with Love* (1957), *Doctor No* (1958), *Goldfinger* (1959), *Thunderball* (1961), *The Spy Who Loved Me* (1962), *On Her Majesty's*

Secret Service (1963), *You Only Live Twice* (1964), and *The Man With the Golden Gun* (1965), and two Bond short story collections: *For Your Eyes Only* (1960) and *Octopussy*—published posthumously—(1966), were released in Britain and America. Critic George Grella states: "Whatever his present standing among readers and critics, Ian Fleming accomplished an extraordinary amount in the history of the thriller. Almost singlehandedly, he revived popular interest in the spy novel, spawning legions of imitations, parodies, and critical and fictional reactions, thus indirectly creating an audience for a number of novelists who followed him in the form."[3] Fleming himself was an English journalist and a Secret Service agent for the British government in 1939, operating under the cover of a journalist for the *London Times* and stationed in Moscow as a reporter. He actually was assigned to the British Foreign Office. Later, he did secret service work as a personal assistant to the Director of Naval Intelligence, all of which gave him considerable material to draw upon for his James Bond series.[4]

Though at the start Fleming had some difficulty getting on the bestseller list with his early Bond novels, by the time of his death in 1964 each new effort sold into the millions of copies, inspiring the longest running series of movies ever produced featuring a single character, and several equally successful Bond pastiches done by other authors, including Kingsley Amis' *Colonel Sun* (1968) and John Gardner's *License Renewed* (1981), *For Special Services* (1982) and *Icebreaker* (1983). Fleming wrote *Casino Royale*, the novel which introduces James Bond, as a distraction from "the shock of getting married at the age of forty-three,"[5] and in 1952 at his home, "Goldeneye," in Oracabessa, Jamaica, penned *Casino Royale*, creating one of the three or four most popular fictional heroes in the world.

Using the plot of Fleming's *Casino Royale* to examine the "good" government versus "evil" government motif complex, the reader finds James Bond, agent of the "good" British Secret Service, assigned to destroy a Soviet spy named Le Chiffre, by beating Le Chiffre at the baccarat tables at the Royale-les-Eaux casino in France. M's dossier (M is head of the British Defence Ministry) on the operation reads as follows:

Subject: A project for the destruction of Monsieur Le Chiffre (alias "The Number," "Herr Nummer," "Herr Ziffer," etc.), one of the Opposition's chief agents in France and undercover Paymaster of the "Syndicat des Ouvriers d'Alsace," the communist controlled trade union in the heavy and transport industries of Alsace and, as we know, an important fifth column in the event of war with Redland.[6]

Le Chiffre, as agent of "Redland," is "evil," not only because he is a communist and a threat to the Allies of post-World War II Europe, but also because he takes delight in being ruthless and savage in his work to the extreme. As the story opens, Le Chiffre is in serious financial troubles since he has invested heavily in a "chain of brothels, known as the 'Cordon Jaune,' operating in Normandy and Brittany," and since France has just passed a law making prostitution illegal. To regain his lost funds before his Soviet overlords discover the loss, Le Chiffre takes to the baccarat tables, there to win a profit of fifty million francs and thus protect his life. By sending Bond, the best gambler in the department, the British Secret Service would rid democracy of a threat, as M's dossier states:

It would be greatly in the interests of this country and of the other nations of the North Atlantic Treaty Organization that this powerful Soviet agent should be ridiculed and destroyed, that his communist trade union should be bankrupted and brought into disrepute, and that this potential fifth column, with a strength of 50,000, capable in time of war of controlling a wide sector of France's northern frontier, should lose faith and cohesion. All this would result if Le Chiffre could be defeated at the tables. (N.B. Assassination is pointless. Leningrad would quickly cover up his defalcations and make him into a martyr.)[7]

As Bond "cases" Le Chiffre at the casino, he notes that the Soviet agent is "a faultless and lucky gambler,"[8] and when he confronts Le Chiffre at the table, he observes Le Chiffre's unsavory physical characteristics: "the unsmiling wet red mouth,"[9] and his automaton-like game playing. But Bond is a better (and as it goes, a luckier) gambler, and he accomplishes his mission by defeating Le Chiffre. The story is not over yet as Le Chiffre, in an attempt to get his money back from Bond, captures Bond's female assistant, Vesper Lynd, thus forcing Bond himself to be captured. The savage side of Le Chiffre's nature emerges as Bond is about to be tortured:

"Perhaps I should explain," said Le Chiffre. "I intend to continue attacking the sensitive parts of your body until you answer my question. I am without mercy, and there will be no relenting. There is no one to stage a last-minute rescue, and there is no possibility of escape for you. This is not a romantic adventure story in which the villain is finally routed and the hero is given a medal and marries the girl. Unfortunately these things don't happen in real life. If you continue to be obstinate, you will be tortured to the edge of madness, and then the girl will be brought in and we will set about her in front of you. If that is still not enough, you will both be painfully killed...."[10]

Fleming is playing with the reader a bit here, having Le Chiffre mock the conventions of the thriller, and since this indeed *is* a "romantic adventure story," Bond does escape the trap with the ironic help of his enemies. A SMERSH agent, a Soviet "hit-man," kills Le Chiffre before he kills Bond, and since the SMERSH agent has no orders to kill anyone but Le Chiffre (for his failure) he lets Bond and Lynd go free. Before Bond is released, the SMERSH agent (as another symbol of savage evil) carves a tattoo on Bond's hand so that he will be known as a spy to other Soviet agents. Throughout the torture scene, Le Chiffre is described as an animal, "snarling like a wild beast," and working "with savage fury." That, and his promise to rape and torture a woman helps to convince the reader of the "evilness," pure and simple, of the villian. This "evidence" is thus applied to his employer, the Soviet Union, and to all that that system of government represents. Evil is equated with communism, and good with Western democracy (symbolized by Bond).

Bond also nicely illustrates the "superhuman" spy motif complex as well. In *Casino Royale,* he is chosen for the mission since he is the "best" gambler. He is a select member of the even more select "OO" section of the British Secret Service (meaning that he has "a license to kill"—for just cause, of course), as well as being handsome, strong and daring. He recognizes his physical limitations, however. When he is observing the casino for the first time, Fleming describes him as always knowing "when his body or his mind had had enough ... thus [helping] him to avoid staleness and the sensual bluntness that breeds mistakes."[12] He knows how to protect himself, how to survive a hostile environment, as shown when he examines the traps that he has set in his room at his hotel: "Doing all this, inspecting these minute burglar-alarms, did not make him feel foolish or self-conscious. He was a secret agent, and still alive thanks to his exact attention to the detail of his profession."[13] He is an expert of fashion and food, as well as being an expert spy, and his missions become exercises of stylish living. He knows more about these things than does the common person (you or I), and the reader is dutifully impressed by the way he does things as much as why he does them. Finally, his treatment of women (sharply contrasted with the villain, Le Chiffre's) defines his charismatic function. Women often fall in love with him (and just as often, if "evil," are morally reformed by him); he is a master of romance. In addition, he is chivalrous to the extreme. When Lynd is captured by Le Chiffre, for example, he debates whether he should go after her:

She was in the Service and knew what she was up against. He wouldn't even ask M. This job was more important than her. It was just too bad. She was a fine girl, but he wasn't going to fall for this childish trick. No dice.[14]

The "realistic" spy would have left Lynd. Bond as the charismatic spy morally cannot. He goes after her, feeling "calm and at ease. The problem of Vesper's life was a problem no longer. His face in the blue light from the [car's] dashboard was grim but serene."[15] After the Le Chiffre affair, Bond and Lynd make love. Disclosed at the story's conclusion is the fact that Lynd is a double-agent, working for the USSR, and reformed by Bond's love for her, she commits suicide rather than disgrace that love. Bond is subsequently motivated further to destroy SMERSH and other evil forces in the world.

The charismatic spy sub-formula of the mystery genre socially defines collective support for Western political ideology. Ideology is held by a group because of specific issues that represent that group's interests.[16] The charismatic spy, as symbol of the virtues of democracy, represents ideological gains at the expense of the wicked and evil Soviets, hence legitimizing the moral superiority of the former as contrasted with the chaotic and destructive nature of the latter. Bond's victories are democracy's victories. It is important to note that in most modern societies there are pluralistic self-interests. This means that they share a core universe of interests as such at a level of mutual accommodation.[17] The charismatic spy story facilitates that mutual accommodation, on a political ideological level, by polarizing Western democracy and Eastern communism into a "good" and "evil" conflict; at a larger political issue, then, unifying pluralistic national interests, saying "though we Western governments have our minor disagreements, we *can* acknowledge that the Soviet sphere is 'bad,' and we must unite to protect against it." And by having the charismatic spy always victorious, it is suggested that good will always triumph over evil, democracy will always triumph over communism.

Politics as Ideological "Soup":
The Dark Spy's Dilemma

LeRoy L. Panek notes that William LeQuex was one of the first authors to "write consistently about espionage."[18] LeQuex (1864-1927) was an artist, journalist and prolific writer of mysteries, about half of which featured spy protagonists. His first novel, *Guilty Bonds* (1891), for example, dealt with the political revolution in Czarist Russia, featuring both spies and counter-spies. Daniel P. King says of LeQuex:

LeQuex gathered much of his background material during his foreign editorship of the *Globe* newspaper (1891-1893) from which he resigned in order to devote his time to writing books. LeQuex had a lively imagination and it is difficult to separate his factual from his fictional works. He often extravagantly embellished situations and presented fiction as fact; he is a perplexing author to assess. He seems to have been involved in the British Secret Service both before and after the First World War and claimed in one of his books to have had an "intimate knowledge of the secret service of continental powers."[19]

It was LeQuex's power to blend fact with fiction, and to illuminate the underside of the spy game, that caused him to be not only one of the first authors to write espionage fiction but to be one of the first to characterize the developing motif complexes of the dark spy sub-formula, those being: 1) the dark spy is an unattractive person who functions as a mere civil servant; 2) the dark spy is morally perplexed by his mission, seeing his own system as neither better nor worse than his adversary's; and 3) the dark spy by fulfilling his assignment, suffers in the process.

The best contemporary example of a dark spy author is John leCarre (1931-   ). LeCarre (pseudonym for David John Moore Cornwell), like Fleming and LeQuex, served as an intelligence officer in the British Secret Service. After World War II, he taught at Eton, later joining the Foreign Service and being assigned to Bonn. His work is described by one critic as "unromantic":

LeCarre's spy novels are not romantic tales of adventure and sex, in the James Bond tradition. His characters are weary victims of the espionage establishment of both sides of the cold war—not supermen, but antiheroes trying to play the game according to the rules and blundering into situations in which they are merely pawns.[20]

John Snyder goes on to say: "John leCarre's realist spy novel is a form which represents a genuine modern version of tragedy: the spy's entrapment through his/her own rationality, by the fate of our time—bureaucratism."[21] LeCarre's most famous novels feature the British Secret Service agent George Smiley and include *Call for the Dead* (1961), *A Murder of Quality* (1962), *The Spy Who Came In From The Cold* (1963), *Tinker, Tailor, Soldier, Spy* (1974) and *The Honourable Schoolboy* (1977).

Smiley is introduced in leCarre's first novel, *Call for the Dead*, and before the action of the story begins, the reader is given a chapter describing Smiley's character. At the start of "Chapter I," we are informed that Smiley's wife, Lady Ann Sercomb, has left him some two years earlier for a Cuban motor racing driver. LeCarre describes Smiley:

Short, fat and of a quiet disposition, he appeared to spend a lot of money on really bad clothes, which hung about his squat frame like skin on a shrunken toad. Sawley, in fact, declared at the wedding that "Sercomb was mated to a bullfrog in a sou'wester." And Smiley, unaware of this description, had waddled down the aisle in search of the kiss that would turn him into a Prince.[22]

Smiley is one of life's nondescript middlemen, who "without wealth or poverty, travelled without labels in the guard's van of the social express, and soon became lost luggage, destined, when the divorce had come and gone, to remain unclaimed on the dusty shelf of yesterday's news."[23] One of Smiley's loves (besides his estranged wife) was "academic excursions into the mystery of human behavior, disciplined by the practical application of his own deductions."[24] Smiley would have been perfectly content to spend his days as an Oxford College Fellow, lecturing on literary obscurities of seventeenth-century Germany, but such was not to be the case for him. Singled out at the university, Smiley was offered a position with the Secret Service, which he accepted, and before the advent of World War II, he worked undercover as a lecturer at a provincial German university, scouting recruits with "the agent potential." This service brought out a dark side of his character:

It intrigued him to evaluate from a detached position what he had learnt to describe as the "agent potential" of a human being; to devise minuscule tests of character and behavior which could inform him of the qualities of a candidate. This part of him was bloodless and inhuman—Smiley in this role was the international mercenary of his trade, amoral and without motive beyond that of personal gratification.[25]

This role, over time, causes Smiley to "witness in himself the gradual death of pleasure,"[26] and to withdraw into himself, avoiding even the happiness of simple friendships:

He learnt what it was never to sleep, never to relax, to feel at any time of day or night the restless beating of his own heart, to know the extremes of solitude and self-pity, the sudden unreasoning desire for a woman, for drink, for exercise, for any drug to take away the tension of his life.[27]

After the War, the Service re-enlists him for new work. Smiley is portrayed as being ugly both physically and morally; and as a representation of the first example of the dark spy motif complex, he is a civil servant who takes pleasure in his amoral ability to label other people's potential to spy. His personal traits are diametrically opposite those of Bond's. Where Bond is attractive to women, Smiley is not. Where Bond is self-assured, Smiley is not. Where Bond is a special "OO" agent, Smiley is a mere bureaucrat. And where Bond lives a life of "romantic individualism," Smiley most certainly does not.

Smiley does not get along well with his superiors. As he is brought

before Maston, the head of his department, to explain if his interview
with another department member, Samuel Arthur Fennan, had caused
that member to commit suicide, Smiley notes that Maston was one of
those civil servants who could "handle paper," who could manage his
staff with the "cumbersome machine of bureaucracy, and who could
reduce any colour to grey."[28] While talking to Maston, Smiley says to
himself: " '[Maston's] weak and frightened. Anyone's neck before [his], I
know. [He is] looking at me that way—measuring me for the rope.' "[29]
And though Smiley tells Maston that his interview with Fennan was a
simple security matter (caused by an anonymous letter denouncing
Fennan as a communist) and that he found no "problems," Maston does
not believe him. Even when Smiley begins to investigate Fennan's
death, and concludes that the suicide was murder, Maston still does not
believe him.

When Smiley goes to check out Fennan's widow concerning the
circumstances of the suicide, Elsa Fennan tells him:

"It's an old illness you suffer from, Mr. Smiley . . . and I have seen many victims
of it. The mind becomes separated from the body; it thinks without reality, rules
a paper kingdom and devises without emotion the ruin of its paper victims."[30]

The deeper Smiley examines this case, learning more to support his
suspicion that Fennan was killed (a wake-up telephone call for the dead
Fennan puts Smiley on the track, hence the novel's title) he also learns
more about his own dissatisfaction with his Secret Service and
government (or any government for that matter). Smiley's journey into
self-doubt, emblematic of the second dark spy motif complex, begins to
reach a climax when he learns that the person behind Fennan's murder
(to cover the fact that Fennan *was* a double-agent) is one of his former
espionage pupils, a German named Dieter Frey whom Smiley recruited
for the Allies during World War II.

As Smiley gets closer to the solution of the mystery, he is physically
beaten and put in the hospital. He also is mentally abused when, at the
story's conclusion, he is fighting with his old student:

Everything he admired or loved had been the product of intense individualism.
That was why he hated Dieter now, hated what he stood for more strongly than
ever before: it was that fabulous impertinence of renouncing the individual in
favor of the mass.[31]

And when he finally kills Dieter in the struggle, Smiley asks in vain why
Dieter did not stop him, did not shoot him with his gun? Again in the
hospital, Smiley contemplates:

Dieter was dead, and he had killed him. The broken fingers of his right hand, the stiffness of his body and the sickening headache, the nausea of guilt, all testified to this. And Dieter had let him do it, had not fired the gun, had remembered their friendship when Smiley had not. They had fought in a cloud, in the rising steam of the river, in a clearing of a timeless forest: they had met, two friends rejoined, and fought like beasts. Dieter had remembered and Smiley had not. They had come from different hemispheres of the night, from different worlds of thought and conduct. Dieter, mercurial, absolute, had fought to build a civilization. Smiley, rationalistic, protective, had fought to prevent him.[32]

The novel closes with Smiley triumphant; he solves the case, kills a communist spy, is offered his job back, yet he is battered physically and mentally, demonstrating the third dark spy motif complex: with success comes suffering.

The dark spy sub-formula, illustrated by leCarre's *Call From the Dead*, narrates a social suspicion of bureaucracy. As evidenced by modern society, the State is ever growingly concerned with the political demands of its own bureaucracy, including of course the establishment of an ideology that supports the bureaucracy.[33] Smiley is suspicious of the system, as the reader, alienated and estranged by the gigantic machinery of bureaucracy, is suspicious of the system. Smiley's feeling of helplessness at the hand of his own government, reflects the reader's feeling of helplessness. And Smiley's recognition of the absurdity of the game of international politics is the reader's as well. The thriller formula presents an intriguing instance where such opposing sub-formulas as the charismatic spy story and the dark spy story can exist and be popular side by side, at the same time for the same audience, suggesting, perhaps, the wonderfully flexible way in which formulas can serve varying social needs (and social perceptions) supplementally.

Notes

[1]LeRoy L. Panek, *The Special Branch: The British Spy Novel, 1890-1980* (Bowling Green: Bowling Green University Popular Press, 1981), p. 282.

[2]*Ibid.*

[3]George Grella, "Ian Fleming," *Twentieth-Century Crime and Mystery Writers*, John M. Reilly, ed., (New York: St. Martin's Press, 1980), p. 571.

[4]Chris Steinbrunner and Otto Penzler, *Encyclopedia of Mystery and Detection* (New York: McGraw-Hill, 1976), pp. 151-152.

[5]Raymond Benson, *The James Bond Bedside Companion* (New York: Dodd, Mead, 1984), p. 3.

[6]Ian Fleming, *Casino Royale* (New York: Signet Books, 1953), p. 13.

[7]*Ibid.*, p. 16.

[8]*Ibid.*, p. 23.

[9]*Ibid.*, p. 61.

[10]*Ibid.*, pp. 93-94.

[11]*Ibid.*, p. 97.

[12]*Ibid.*, p. 7.

[13]*Ibid.*, pp. 11-12.

[14]*Ibid.*, p. 82.

[15]*Ibid.*, p. 83.

[16]Peter L. Berger and Thomas Luckmann, *The Social Construction of Reality* (Garden City: Doubleday, 1966), p. 124.

[17]*Ibid.*, p. 125.

[18]Panek, p. 5.

[19]Daniel P. King, "William LeQuex," *Twentieth-Century Crime and Mystery Writers*, John M. Reilly, ed., (New York: St. Martin's Press, 1980), p. 944.

[20]Steinbrunner and Penzler, p. 242.

[21]John Snyder, "John leCarre," *Twentieth-Century Crime and Mystery Writers*, John M. Reilly, ed., (New York: St. Martin's Press, 1980), p. 933.

[22]John leCarre, "Call for the Dead," *The Incongruous Spy* (New York: Walker, 1961), p. 7.

[23]*Ibid.*, p. 8.

[24]*Ibid.*, p. 11.

[25]*Ibid.*

[26]*Ibid.*

[27]*Ibid.*, p. 13.

[28]*Ibid.*, p. 14.

[29]*Ibid.*, p. 21.

[30]*Ibid.*, p. 30.

[31]*Ibid.*, p. 169.

[32]*Ibid.*, p. 178.

[33]Peter L. Berger, *The Sacred Canopy: Elements of a Sociological Theory of Religion* (Garden City: Doubleday, 1967) pp. 132-133.

CHAPTER VIII
Detective Formula

Rationalism and Detection:
The Classical Detective

AT THE MOST RATIONAL END of the mystery genre spectrum, to the right still of the thriller story, is the detective formula. The detective hero was first invented by Edgar Allan Poe, and with that invention, in a type of formulaic full-circle movement, the classical detective sub-formula gained its inspiration, in part from the Gothic tradition.

From the death of Descartes in 1650 through the death of Hume in 1776, there established in European thought an Age of Enlightenment in which the mechanistic Newtonian model became an overriding metaphor, and in which scientific experimentation founded on empiricism became the basis for philosophical self-confidence.[1] This paradigm, apparently, eventually became intellectually stifling for the European upper and middle classes, and soon gave way to the Romantic movement: in popular literature, spearheaded by the advent of the Gothic novel. As we have noted, the literary universe of the Gothic threw the human-manipulated mechanism of social control to the four winds as novel after lurid novel was published featuring moaning ghosts drifting through dark corridors of hidden torture-chambers enforcing divine, supernatural maledictions.

Edgar Allan Poe (1809-1849) successfully aided in transplanting the Gothic story from Europe to America, and in addition to being a major literary critic and one of the first American authors to write fantasy, science fiction and psychological suspense stores, he nurtured a reputation on such Gothic tales as "Ligeia" (1838) and "The Fall of the House of Usher" (1839). In "Usher," for example, one rediscovers several of the motif complexes first established by Walpole in *The Castle of Otranto*: the crumbling mansion infused with a melancholic sense of the supernatural and human-inspired aberrations of nature. Whether "Usher" is interpreted as a tale of insanity or the supernatural, the basic confrontation between the individual and a hostile universe nevertheless concludes in like fashion. The individual's own action and intellect, those qualities so important to the European Age of Enlightenment, are meaningless when exposed to various natural or supernatural elements beyond his personal control. The raging storm in the Gothic, as an agent of Fate, often destroys or maims the hero and villain alike, and the only chance for physical or mental survival is submission to that Fate. Thus, as an example of Poe's use of the Gothic sub-formula in "Usher," the final passage of the story defines the individual's sense of helplessness when challenged by the cosmic:

From that chamber, and from that mansion, I fled aghast. The storm was still abroad in all its wrath as I found myself crossing the old causeway. Suddenly, there shot along the path a wild light, and I turned to see whence a gleam so unusual could have issued; for the vast house and its shadows were alone behind me. The radiance was that of the full, setting and blood-red moon which now shone vividly through that once barely-discernible fissure of which I have spoken as extending from the roof of the building, in a zig-zag direction, to the base. While I gazed, this fissure widened—there came a fierce breath of the whirlwind—the entire orb of the satellite burst at once upon my sight—my brain reeled as I saw the mighty walls rushing asunder—there was a long tumultuous shouting sound like the voice of a thousand waters—and the deep and dark tarn at my feet closed sullenly and silently over the fragments of the "House of Usher."[2]

Any enactment of human-inspired aberration of nature in the Gothic, as with Manfred's betrayal of his wife's loyalty in *The Castle of Otranto*, or as with Roderick Usher's possible incestuous relationship with his sister Madeline in "Usher," results in the total destruction of the transgressor's sense of being or importance. There is little chance for forgiveness and almost certain chance of havoc.

-    Poe is posthumously remembered not just for his successful excursions into the Gothic sub-formula, however, for with his publication of "The Murders in the Rue Morgue" (*Graham's Magazine*, 1841), he developed a new mystery sub-formula that took the genre in new directions in both Europe and America. Though "Murders" possesses all the trappings of a Gothic shocker—including the expected foreboding mansions, and human and supernatural-inspired aberrations of nature leading to grotesque situations (death and murder)—Poe's contribution to the genre was the creation of an uncommonly intelligent hero, a metaphoric representation of the Age of Enlightenment, a character who could set the wrongs of evil in a proper moral cast (thus subsuming divine will into his own will), and who reinforces the security of social institutions against the threat of criminal anarchy and violence via the process of rational manipulations of the environment. Poe's Monsieur C. Auguste Dupin thus became the first modern detective hero, and the prototype for the first of the four sub-formulas of the detective formula: the classical detective.

Poe founded three motif complexes of the classical detective story in "The Murders in the Rue Morgue": 1) the detective is a character emblematic of pure reason; he is the most intelligent person in the story who possesses an extraordinary ability to locate "clues" (or facts) that eventually disclose truth; 2) the crime, or "mystery," functions as a puzzle where the pieces (clues) are assembled by the detective, hence suggesting an intellectual (rather than physical) exercise of the conflict between the individual and his environment; and 3) every mystery, no matter how bizarre or irrational, has a rational solution, suggesting a fictional world where the individual controls Fate, possesses free will and conquers his environment.

Poe spends a good amount of time prefacing "Murders" with a discussion of intelligence, differentiating "simple ingenuity" from "analytical power," the latter being a superior intellectual exercise since it includes imagination. Auguste Dupin, as Poe's example of the first motif complex of classical detective fiction, is analytical, and thus of a superior human intellect. As the narrator meets Dupin, at an obscure library in the Rue Montmarte in Paris searching for the same "obscure volume," they strike a friendship. The narrator is astonished at the "vast extent of Dupin's reading [and, most importantly] at the vivid freshness of his imagination."[3] They decide to room together in a "grotesque mansion, long deserted through superstition," called the Faubourg St. Germain.[4] There, in a pseudo-supernatural setting (as a defiance of the supernatural), Dupin and the narrator establish a home base from which to wander the streets of Paris at night, and to begin their intellectual battle with crime. The narrator notes about Dupin:

... I could not help remarking and admiring...a peculiar analytic ability in Dupin. He seemed, too, to take an eager delight in its exercise—if not exactly in its display—and did not hesitate to confess the pleasure thus derived. He boasted to me, with a low chuckling laugh, that most men, in respect to himself, wore windows in their bosoms, and was wont to follow up such assertions by direct and very startling proofs of his intimate knowledge of my own.[5]

Dupin, after demonstrating to the narrator and to the reader the power of his analytical ability, notices an interesting, if not baffling crime in the evening edition of the paper. A woman and her daughter have been horribly murdered in their home at the Rue Morgue, with no apparent motive or method. Dupin takes the case as a challenge, and by closely examining the clues (which no one else, of course, notices) and by the process of analytical deduction (which no one else, of course, can accomplish—including the police) he solves the mystery, naming the murderer as an escaped pet ourang-outang that climbed into the victims' window, killed them and escaped. The ape belonged to a sailor, who as Dupin surmises, is summoned to Dupin when the detective places an ad in the paper advertising the lost animal. When the sailor arrives, Dupin confronts him with the truth, and demands the story. After all the facts of the case have been settled, Dupin comments:

"I am satisfied with having defeated him [the Prefect Police] in his own castle. Nevertheless, that he failed in the solution of this mystery, is by no means the matter for wonder which he supposes it; for in truth, our friend the Prefect is somewhat too cunning to be profound."

Thus Dupin, as mentally superior to the narrator (who functions as a foil to Dupin's abilities) and to the police, assembles the facts of the mystery and reveals the truth.

For Dupin (and for the reader), the murders and the circumstances surrounding those murders, are reduced during the telling of the story to a game, specifically a puzzle which is intellectually pieced together by Dupin (and the reader) over the course of the action, illustrating the second classical detective motif complex. Dupin is the master game player who is more than just a game player. He is a character who can invite the reader's empathy while at the same time marshaling a society's cultural perceptions of right, morality and goodness around his presence. The classical detective, Dupin, is much more than a literary agent of the cheap thrill, of the pleasant intellectual diversion that entertains, amuses and passes time. The puzzle of the classical detective story serves as a symbol in society for the cultural dialectic that operates in all forms of popular fiction and furthermore in every form of cultural expression, the cultural dialectic which illustrates the polarized tension between the ever-changing and ever-constant, between the social perception and the cultural archetype. The archetypal interest of this sub-formula is not concerned with what is accepted or unaccepted in society. It is concerned with what is legally and morally forbidden, specifically with certain aspects of social taboo. The social construction of reality moderates the creation of the classical detective hero who enforces taboo structures in society, and this process becomes embodied as the puzzle. The hero's generic appellation implies the process of detection, the detection of crime, the detection of criminals—and the detection of social taboos (the cultural archetype). The detective, during the game, while solving the puzzle, searches for information and discovers not only the means, method and motive of the crime and criminal, but the relationship between aberrant individual and society. Classical detective fiction stages a morality game: the subject of the contest revolves around an individual's violation of taboo (murder, theft) and society's reaction (embodied in that "super-ambassador of society": the classical detective) to that violation. By successfully completing the game, by successfully solving the crime puzzle, Dupin functions as a doctor to society, who eliminates the cancer of society (individual aberration) and restores the validity of taboo structure within the culture.

By suggesting that every crime, or mystery, is a puzzle which has a rational solution, the third classical detective motif complex, this sub-formula implies that the individual controls his own life (is not manipulated by supra-human others) and thus can control society's problems (like crime). Rationality suggests that all human activity has an historical context to govern it; thus personal fortune and misfortune are products of individual action.[7] Therefore if crime is invented by people, it can be eliminated by people's actions. If death is not the product of supernature (as in the supernatural formula), or a hostile Fate (as in the fiction noir formula), then death can be prevented by the individual. Granted, this requires the best hero that society can produce, but nonetheless this hero is human, is free from divine influence and is capable of directing a socially positive outcome (the elimination of crime and criminals) solely through his own efforts.

Since Poe's Dupin, over the years a number of popular mystery writers have worked effectively within the classical detective sub-formula including Sir Arthur Conan Doyle, Agatha Christie, John Dickson Carr and Dorothy Sayers. As they refined the sub-formula, they also enhanced and popularized its social function, specifically with regard to plot structure. The substance of the plot in this sub-formula, as mentioned above, is anti-social behavior, and as dramatized in every contribution to the development of the classical detective story, the fictional catalyst which motivates the hero's act of detecting revolves around three levels of taboo violations. At the most basic level, the role of the criminal serves as a social definition of what is unacceptable behavior. He *is* a criminal because his individual accomplishments enter taboo areas. He is a murderer, a thief, a liar and the detailing of his actions defines society's objections to and limits of taboo violation. For example, it is culturally acceptable in classical detective fiction to kill an individual in self-defense. However, if one plots the killing of a person for purposes of revenge, financial gain or sexual gratification, a culturally accepted act becomes unacceptable and falls into the realm of taboo. Thus is defined the difference between hero and villain, between taboo enforcer and taboo breaker. At the next level, the objects of interest in classical detective fiction, icons of wealth and power, function as symbols of fulfillment of the myth of material success. Money, jewelry, stocks, art treasures, these things are immensely desirable for members of a large middle-class readership, unless, of course, they are acquired by acts of unacceptable violence or theft. Unless taboos are observed in the acquisition of such wealth, the sub-formula reminds us, then swift and powerful sanctions soon follow. Finally, as illustrated above, the classical detective hero is created as an example of how intellectual control can dominate anarchism. If the criminal represents a type of social hoodlum, an aggressively amoral character who over-indulges his more primitive urges, then the classical detective, as a creature of emotionless reason, suggests in an allegorical manner how the unswerving ritual of observation, detection and discovery can solve seemingly irrational violations of taboo. Ultimately, the classical detective argues the most radical separation of emotion and reason in taboo maintenance, and the culmination of social justice rests upon the hero's successful manipulation of mental resources and defiance of rampant emotional individualism.

The System and Detection:
The Police Detective

The next historical development within the detective formula, after Poe's invention of the classical detective hero, is the creation of the police detective hero. Elements of the police detective sub-formula began to unfold even before Poe, however, in the work of Vidocq. Francois Eugene Vidocq's four-volume *Memories*, published in France between 1886 and 1929, though claimed by Vidocq to be "factual," constitute the first examples of the police detective sub-formula. Vidocq (1775-1857) was a French detective and founder of the Police de Surete. Early in his life he had a miltary career, though later he entered a life of crime and ended up in prison. In 1809 he offered Napoleon his services as a criminal informer, and over a period of time, finally became the first chief of the police department.[8] Vidocq's *Memories* were thought to be ghostwritten. However, at the time of their publication (in France, Britain and the U.S.) they were taken as the authentic documents of Vidocq's career as a policeman. As fiction, they evidence several motif complexes of the police detective sub-formula that were to be more widely employed by modern mystery writers: 1) the police detective uses "systematic" methods of police work to investigate crime; and 2) the policeman is a symbol of the system itself, and who, by "going by the book," accomplishes his task (as being merely a job done by any civil servant).

In looking at "Victims of My Craft," an excerpt from *Memories*, the reader quickly notes the episodic frame of the story. This structure is fairly common to most police detective stories, where the policeman encounters a problem, then solves that problem, encounters another problem and solves that, and over the course of the narrative, works on several cases rather than one. Historian of the police procedural George N. Dove calls this the "Dragnet" type of story (based on the television show's story formula).[9] The implication in this kind of structure is that police work, rather than being an apocalyptic battle with crime (as it is with the avenger detective sub-formula), or a massive puzzle which "freezes" the activities of the police until the mental "superman" solves the puzzle and sets society straight (as in the classical sub-formula), or part of a larger, organized conspiracy to collect graft from helpless citizens (as in the hard-boiled sub-formula), is instead indicative of the rather workmanlike nature of policing, of the "plain-job-which-needs-to-be-finished" kind of tale.

One systematic police method in "Victims," from the first smaller episode of crime in which Vidocq is hunting for the counterfeiter, Watrin, is surveillance of the criminal setting. As Vidocq describes it:

... I began to pound the pavement in order to become familiar with it and to be able to do my work usefully. These excursions, during the course of which I made a great number of observations, took me twenty days, during which I was only preparing myself to act; I was studying the terrain.[10]

The police detective requires time and patience to accomplish his work. His success against crime lies more in the ability to be persistent than in any great, sudden analytical "break-through." The police detective discovers his clues by going over and over again the subject of his search. Vidocq further illustrates this aspect of police work:

I lay in wait near-by night and day in order to have an eye on the comings and goings. This supervision had lasted nearly a week. Finally, tired of seeing nothing, I conceived the idea of getting the master of the house in my interests and hiring an apartment.[11]

Thus, two systematic police methods are the stake-out and the police detective's ability to disguise himself (not in the melodramatic fashion of the spy or the avenger detective, but plainly, unobtrusively). After his capture of Watrin, Vidocq is on the prowl for an even bigger crook, Saint-Germain. He constantly pursues Saint-Germain, always keeping an eye on him to see what sort of crime he will pull next, hence offering a further police method: the tailing of the criminal to the crime. These instances of the first motif complex of police detective fiction underscore the fact that the policeman is a professional (not a vigilante as is the avenger detective, or an amateur as is the classical detective), a specialist of crime. Given the accumulation of knowledge in society, division of labor is necessary, and the specialization of knowledge will be easier to gather quickly for the individual than generalized knowledge. Bureaucracy creates specialized tasks which, in turn, require specialized knowledge of certain situations, and of the causal relationships of those situations.[12] Specialists, like the police detective hero, will arise, each to fulfill his task,[13] such as the catching of the crook. This sub-formula, thus, allows the reader to examine the methods of the professional specialist, to see how the system works, and more importantly to see *that* the system works.

In the end, of course, Vidocq leads his fellow police to Saint-Germain, and there in a gun battle captures him. Says Vidocq: "I remember no event in my life which brought me more joy than the capture of Saint-Germain. I applauded myself for having delivered society from this monster."[14] Vidocq senses pride in his accomplishments and in seeing how the police system works so well in catching the "big fish" of crime. This second motif complex of the police detective sub-formula is reaffirmed with the creation of the first modern example of the police hero in American culture, Chester Gould's comic strip character, *Dick Tracy*. Started in 1931, the strip has outlasted the life of its inventor, continuing in popularity up to the present, and it recounts Tracy's fight against vile gangsters like Pruneface, Flattop, the Brow and the Mole. Gould took great care to document actual police methods so that he could include these in his comic's scripts. Tracy is *always* triumphant with his "war on crime;" hence the system is always capable of dealing with the social misfits of evil. However, with the publication of Lawrence Treat's novel, *V as in Victim* (1945), this second motif complex began to change:

Treat's *V as in Victim*... introduced a new way of dealing with the police story. The cops bore the burden of detection, but they were not "heroes," nor did they display any suggestion of awe-inspiring powers of ratiocination. For the most part they worked in teams, using the methodology normally employed by policemen in real life.[15]

Police detective novels started to appear in which the cop is unhappy, or alienated, by the system, in which he must encounter the drudgery (and sometimes violent danger) of his work with the same sort of disfavor that he encounters crime. The police officer, as exampled in

Joseph Wambaugh's work, is acted upon, rather than acting upon the criminal forces of society. David K. Jeffrey says of Wambaugh's *The Choirboys*:

Wambaugh also examines the psychic cost of police work in *The Choirboys*, but he does so with a broad and bawdy comic technique reminiscent of *Catch-22*. The novel includes a series of hilarious episodes depicting incompetent, high-ranking officers and alcoholic, claustrophobic, masochistic, sadistic, and vampiric policemen.... The juxtaposition suggests how and why police work taints a cop's vision of others and of himself; it suggests as well how some policemen try to cope with horror.[16]

A sociological aspect of alienation suggests that the individual creates a world, through the social construction of reality, that denies its creator.[17] It is this process, the police detective enforcing the laws of a society which turn back upon him to alienate him, that has provided the dilemma plot substance for not only Wambaugh, but for Georges Simenon (Joseph Christian) and Ed McBain, two other modern masters of the sub-formula, as well.

Individualism and Detection:
The Hard-Boiled Detective

After the classical and police sub-formulas, the hard-boiled sub-formula evolved as a product of the American pulp magazines, specifically the detective pulp, *Black Mask*. *Black Mask* was originally intended by its founders, H.L. Mencken and George Jean Nathan, to be a "profit-maker" that would make solvent another Mencken/Nathan pulp title, *The Smart Set* (which was having some financial troubles).[18] These publishers had no doubt seen the commercial success of Street and Smith's detective pulp, *Detective Story*, and had noted that crime, perhaps, does indeed "pay." Writing to a friend, Ernest Boyd, in 1919, Mencken says of *Black Mask's* creation: "I am thinking of venturing into a new cheap magazine scheme .... The opportunity is good and we need the money."[19] And when *Black Mask* first appeared on American newsstands in 1920, it primarily featured rather traditional classical detective fare. The pulp changed publishers and editorial hands several times between 1920 and 1923, but by the May 15, 1923 issue, under the direction of editor George W. Sutton Jr., with the publication of Carroll John Daly's short story "Three Gun Terry," the classical detective content of the magazine began to be replaced by a new detective sub-formula, the hard-boiled story.[20]

Carroll John Daly, then, is the father of the hard-boiled private eye.[21] Daly began tinkering with the hard-boiled character in two earlier stories in *Black Mask*: "The False Burton Combs" (December 1922), in which appears a protagonist who is a "soldier of fortune" and who makes his living by "working against the law breakers;"[22] and "It's All in the Game" (April 15, 1923), in which the protagonist works under the disguise of a private detective for his illegal, crime-fighting activities.[23] But it is with "Three Gun Terry" that the hard-boiled detective hero first claimed membership in the detective formula.

Daly (1889-1958) was a prolific writer of detective fiction and sold a great number of stories to a variety of pulp titles. His most famous hard-boiled hero was Race Williams, and in addition to publishing this series character in an assortment of pulps, he featured Williams in several hardcover novels, including *The Snarl of the Beast* (1927), *The Hidden Hand* (1929), *The Tag Murders* (1930), *Tainted Power* (1931), *The Third Murderer* (1931), *The Amateur Murderer* (1933), *Murder from the East* (1935) and *Better Corpses* (1940). Daly also wrote several other popular series hard-boiled detective heroes, such as Vee Brown, Clay Holt and Satan Hall, the last named finding his way into two hardcover publications with *The Mystery of the Smoking Gun* (1935) and *Ready to Burn* (1951). *Black Mask* scholar William F. Nolan says of Daly's writing, however:

From the outset of his career in 1922, to the end of his productivity in the mid-1950s, Daly remained an artificial, awkward, self-conscious pulpster, endlessly repetitious, hopelessly melodramatic. He had absolutely no ability for three-dimensional characterization nor did he possess a feel for language or mood.[24]

The question of Daly's artistic style aside, he nonetheless inspired imitation by other "more gifted" hard-boiled authors, like Dashiell Hammett and Raymond Chandler, and he laid the frame for the hard-boiled motif complexes of, first, the tough, individualistic detective hero, and, second, the dangerous, corrupt urban environment in which the hard-boiled detective must solve his mysteries.

In "Three Gun Terry," with respect to the first sub-formula motif complex, the protoganist, Terry Mack, describes his personal philosophy:

My life is my own, and the opinions of others don't interest me; so don't form any, or if you do, keep them to yourself. If you want to sneer at my tactics, why go ahead; but do it behind the pages—you'll find that healthier.[25]

Terry is a strong individualist, to the point of challenging the reader to question his methods. His talk is tough, as are his actions. He hits harder, shoots faster and is more able to endure punishment than are his adversaries, and as the term "hard-boiled" implies, the more pressure Mack is put under, the tougher he becomes. Mack continues to tell the reader about his character, saying:

I ain't a crook, and I ain't a dick; I play the game on the level, in my own way. I'm the center of a triangle; between crook and the police and the victim. The police have had an eye on me for some time, but only an eye, never a hand; they don't get my lay at all. The crooks; well, some is on, and some ain't; most of them don't know what to think, until I've put the hooks in them. When it comes to shooting, I don't have to waste time cleaning my gun.[26]

Mack is neither crook nor cop, but instead observes his own code of conduct. Rather than being portrayed as a symbol of justice for urban society, Mack (and other hard-boiled detective heroes) serves as an emblem of personal honor ("I play the game on the level," Mack says), a knight operating within a social structure of civic corruption and hostility ("they don't get my lay at all," Mack tells us), decadence and dishonesty. But rather than resorting to the tactics of the bad gangster or the bad thief to survive, the hard-boiled detective hero lives his life as he sees fit ("in my own way," Mack says). Part of that personal code of conduct includes women, and often the hero of the hard-boiled story is drawn into a mystery to either protect the vulnerable female figure or to be used by the "evil" female figure. Mack, in "Three Gun Terry" starts the case by rushing to help a woman who is being kidnapped by three gunmen. He rationalizes to the reader that "there probably would be jack [money] in this for yours truly,"[27] but we smell-out his bluff (knowing there are better, more sure-fire ways to make money) and recognize his metaphoric "suit of white armour." The rescue of the woman, Nita, and her return to her "family," start the hard-boiled detective hero down a path to investigate a greater, more terrible crime. Nita's "uncle" (a villain, the reader later discovers) employs Mack to locate a missing sheet of paper containing a "formula." Naturally, Mack locates the formula, uncovers the layers of deceit surrounding the manipulation of his efforts to place the formula (for the composition of a deadly poison gas to be used for military purposes) in the criminal's grasp and collects the crooks, all through his tough, individual efforts. Noting the sociological function of the concept of individualism, the ability to be individualistic is correlated to unsuccessful socialization.[28] Mack, as an individual, recognizes the problems of society and refuses to be socialized by that society. Society is hence suspicious and hostile to someone who does not "play their game."

Which brings us to the second hard-boiled motif complex. At the start of "Three Gun Terry," Mack enters the city streets to look for business:

Now, the city's big, and that ain't meant for no outburst of personal wisdom. It's fact. Sometimes things is slow and I go out looking for business. About the cabarets; in the big hotels and even along the streets I find it. It's always there. I just spot some well-known faces playing their suckers, and that's my change.[29]

Mack not only finds business in the streets; he finds evil also. The denizens of those streets play their suckers, as Mack says, but the city itself plays its inhabitants as suckers as well. Unlike the classical sub-formula (where the city is a symbol of order) in the hard-boiled story the city is no longer a place worth defending. It is a dark, dangerous environ, the abode of murderers and thieves, organized by political grafters who operate at every level of government. New York, Chicago, Los Angeles, the names of these cities become euphemisms for evil. Often the hard-boiled hero is beaten by agents of society, and his health serves as a peculiar sacrifice for the sins of the city as he is battered from chapter to chapter in his heroic quest for truth. The detective in the hard-boiled story, rather than being the moral criminal (as the criminal-as-radical-individual is portrayed in the classical sub-formula), is instead the last bastion of honor in an amoral world that has lost all sense of moral meaning. The hard-boiled hero will not be coerced by a social system that legitimizes itself by criminal activity. There is a devious method by which society claims validity; it wants to suggest that it has existed since the beginning of time. By letting its members believe that obeying its laws (in the hard-boiled story, playing by corrupt rules) will place them within the legitimized order of the cosmos, it insures its perpetuation.[30] The hard-boiled detective hero, however, knows that this order of the universe is devil-controlled, and he does not want to be a devil's pawn. The hero's solution of the case, of getting at the truth, is but a smaller reflection of the hero's solution of the mystery of society.

Two of the more famous authors to write within the hard-boiled sub-formula are Dashiell Hammett and Raymond Chandler. Hammett (1894-1961) penned a number of short stories and novels featuring his "nameless" private-eye: the Continental Op. The Op appeared in the novels *Red Harvest* (1929), *The Dain Curse* (1929) and *The Big Knock-Over* (1948). *The Maltese Falcon* (1930) was the only novel to highlight Hammett's most renowned detective, *Sam Spade*, and *The Thin Man* (1934) and *The Glass Key* (1931) complete the list of his longer fiction. Author Robert B. Parker says of the above material:

And what are the novels about? They are about men who persist in the face of adversity until they do what they set out to do. They are about men who have few friends and no permanent social context. Except for Ned Beaumont in *The Glass Key* these men are detectives. Except for Nick Charles in *The Thin Man* they are alone. They have no family. Their allegiance is not to law but to something else, call it order, a sense of the way things ought to be. They are not of the police any more than they are of the mob.[31]

Chandler (1888-1959) placed his hard-boiled detective, Philip Marlowe, in all his novels: *The Big Sleep* (1939), *Farewell, My Lovely* (1940), *The High Window* (1942), *The Lady in the Lake* (1944), *The Little Sister* (1949), *The Long Goodbye* (1953) and *Playback* (1958). Parker, again, critiques Chandler's work by stating:

[Marlowe] is a man of honor .... Honor has several virtues. It may be maintained in defeat as well as triumph .... In a dishonorable world, to persist in honorable behavior is to court adversity .... Whether or not we admire Marlowe's ideals, his willingness to incur injury and risk death rather than forsake them invests both his ideals and his behavior with moral seriousness.[32]

Like the classical detective and police detective sub-formulas, the hard-boiled story continues to thrive to the present, finding strength and "new blood" from various media adaptations (especially in television and film) and because of the efforts of such hard-boiled writers as Hammett and Chandler, the formula of detective fiction has gained new respectability among the otherwise adverse critics and detractors of popular fiction worldwide.

Violence and Detection:
The Avenger Detective
The last major contribution to the detective formula was the avenger detective sub-formula. As did the charismatic spy story, the avenger detective sub-formula saw its start in the American dime novel, in particular with the character Nick Carter. Nick Carter was the perfect example of the perfect (late 1800s) detective. Dime novel publisher (later to become pulp publisher) Street and Smith commissioned a host of "house" authors, including Frederick Van Rensselaer Dey and John Russell Coryell, to write countless Nick Carter adventures. The sheer amount of Nick Carter dime novel fiction published was staggering (even by today's mass media standards). From his first published account, *The Old Detective Pupil, or The Mysterious Crime of Madison Square*, serialized in the *New York Weekly* (September 1886), to the first actual extended series of Nick Carter adventures, the *Nick Carter*

Library, which began publication in 1891 (and ran for 282 issues), to the longest running Nick Carter series, the *New Nick Carter Weekly*, which began in 1897 (and this time ran for 819 issues), and on to *Nick Carter Stories, New Magnet* and *Street and Smith's Detective Story Magazine*, the total amount of Nick Carter dime novels printed must have reached into the millions of copies. To this day, no one has really calculated exactly how many Carter issues were published.

Nick Carter began his career at the tender age of twenty-four. He was first introduced to his reading public as "the world's greatest detective," and he found little argument for that title among his fictional contemporaries. He was literally born into his job, being the son of Sim Carter, a "great" detective in his own right. Nick was often described as the "little Hercules." He was called "little" because he was a relatively short man. Of course, what he lacked in size he more than made up for in strength, courage and intelligence. He gave true meaning to the term "superman." Virtually *nothing* was outside the abilities of this amazing powerhouse. He could bend a bar of iron in his bare hands. He could run faster, climb higher and throw farther than anyone else during his time or since. Nick Carter became the by-word vernacular for the best that was humanly possible.

A serious problem developed in the writing of the Nick Carter series, something perhaps totally unexpected by the series' writers and editors: Nick Carter was *too* powerful a hero. No common crook could stand up for very long against the might and intelligence of the "little Hercules." This problem was eventually solved with the creation of a villain whose powers and abilities rivaled the hero's own, a "supervillain," if you will. Doctor Jack Quartz thus became Nick Carter's single greatest adversary, appearing in many of Carter's adventures. Dr. Quartz was a criminal mastermind, as well as a skilled surgeon and scientist. Often portrayed as being of medium height, clean-shaven and a little portly, he was nearly as strong as Nick himself. Interestingly, both hero and villain held great respect for each other throughout their adventures. Perhaps skill and genius were sympathetic skill and genius, no matter which side of the law they were on.

Thus, with the Nick Carter series, two motif complexes of the avenger detective sub-formula evolved: first, that the avenger detective hero is a person of great strength, intelligence and courage who works outside the law to protect the law from its own limitations; and second that the conflict between the avenger detective and his "supervillain" adversary recounts, at a basic level, a larger, apocalyptic conflict between relatively evenly-matched forces of good and evil.

As the early years of the Great Depression began to exert their economic impact on American society, the classical detective started to offer less relevance for a popular American reading audience, and thus the avenger detective hero, first begun in detective dime novels of the mid-1880s some four decades earlier, emerged in the popular press and radio to captivate the nation's fancy by effectively solving criminal problems with vigilante violence. The avenger detective hero catered to the societal desire for simplified solutions to complex situations. With the publication of the April 1931 issue of Street and Smith's *Shadow Magazine*, the first of the Depression-era vigilante pulp magazines, the twin motif complexes of the sub-formula were resurrected for the consumption of a new generation. In the mid-1930s, a radio program entitled *Detective Story Program* featured an announcer known mysteriously as "The Shadow" who dramatized material from a pulp magazine. Street and Smith publishers, possessing that strong tradition of marketing mass media heroes during the dime novel era, recognized a potential commercial property and decided, in 1931, to launch *The Shadow Magazine*.[33] Walter Gibson was contracted to write the first Shadow adventure, more to secure the copyright of the radio personality than anything else, and writing under the pseudonym of "Maxwell Grant" Gibson produced the novel *The Living Shadow*, though not without some difficulties. Gibson remarks that after writing the early chapters of *The Living Shadow*, he was asked to re-write them, introducing a "Chinese angle," somehow tying-in a man in Chinese costume: "clutching an upraised hand that cast a huge shadow on the wall behind him."[34] When *The Shadow* hit the newsstands, it touched that Depression readership effectively, and sold out. A second and a third novel nearly sold out, and Street and Smith decided the demand was strong enough to warrant the magazine becoming a monthly rather than a quarterly publication. Even with a novel a month, readers still clamored for more stories. With the October 1, 1932 issue, *The Shadow Magazine* was released as a bi-weekly and remained that way through March 1, 1943. The magazine continued publication to the summer of 1949, eventually totaling 325 Shadow adventures, most of which were written by Gibson. Concurrently, the Shadow continued his presence on the radio, becoming one of the most popular detective/adventure radio heroes of the Depression years. What had begun as a simple copyright practice quickly blossomed into a media event, because it supplied something heroic that the public needed, the extent of this need being reflected in the speed with which that public bought the issues and in the reliability with which they listened to the radio programs.

Street and Smith decided to duplicate their "luck" and in March, 1933 published the first *Doc Savage Magazine* (featuring the novel *The Man of Bronze*). Though not quite as successful as the Shadow, the *Doc Savage Magazine* continued publication through the summer of 1949, telling some 181 adventures. With the near instant success of the Shadow and Doc Savage, other publishers released their own hero pulp magazines—with dollar signs gleaming in their eyes—and between 1931 and 1949, some fifty-six different avenger titles appeared.[35] The heroes of those magazines included characters like the Avenger, Captain Satan, the Moon Man, Operator 5, the Phantom Detective, Secret Agent X and the Spider.

After 1931 dozens of pulp avenger detectives heroes laughed, whispered, battled and killed their way through the fictional "mean streets" of Depression America. One aspect of the Depression WASP mindset was the radically conservative—even reactionary—attitude held towards criminals and crime in the avenger detective pulp magazine sub-formula. In these stories, traditional law enforcement agencies are unable to deal with crime; thus the avenger detective hero adopts vigilantism (as a personal, moral quest for justice) to deal with the problem. If the crook is menacing society and threatens destruction of law and order, the hero of this sub-formula presents a simple, conservative solution—kill the enemy.

Most of the villains of the avenger detective pulps represent the bottom rung of the social ladder. They are foreigners, the ethnics, and the hardened unemployed. The "supervillains" of these stories are symbolic socialists and communists who literally adopt the "share the wealth" worldview of their Marxist ideological predecessors. Though they undeniably crave personal wealth and power, they nonetheless employ that element of society that is shunned. The "supervillain" offers, formulaically, a type of liberal social reform that was distasteful for a middle-class Depression readership. The pulp avenger detective hero, as the fictional agent of extreme conservatism, inexorably "gets his man" before the devil of economic insanity overthrows the virtuous capitalistic power structure. The "supervillain," as social reformer, offered an unsure, an insecure and unacceptable future, while the pulp avenger detective offered the promise of a secure WASP conservatism, the same "stuff" (metaphorically) that made America "great" in the first place. As a vigilante figure who employs violence to protect the system, the avenger detective hero in these stories becomes a sociological symbol of the way violence is used to secure the institutions of political life. Every institution is forced to confront the problems of power, and hence allocates that power to individuals through political institutions.[36] When power is not properly regulated, political breakdowns happen. The avenger detective hero uses violence, an otherwise socially unacceptable method of power manipulation, to reinforce the structure of society, ironically, to break the rules of society to save society. Thus is evidenced the popularity of this sub-formula's first motif complex.

The threat of the criminal to society assumed epic proportions in avenger detective pulp magazines. Super-criminals endanger the lives and fortunes of great numbers of helpless people, not just certain selected individuals (as in the classical sub-formula), and law enforcement agencies themselves, seen merely as incompetent in classical detective fiction, crumble against the "supervillains" of this sub-formula. Thus, the fabric of crime in these stories is woven of apocalyptic thread. Walter Gibson, the main writer of the Shadow series character, describes the relationship of the Shadow with his adversaries:

As his [the Shadow's] forays expanded, the Shadow came into conflict with formidable antagonists, whose own cryptic identities became the titles for the stories in which most of them met their deserved doom, notably, *The Silent Seven, The Black Master, The Crime Cult* and *Six Men of Evil*. These involved spy rings, murder cults, mad scientists, and haunted houses .... At times, the Shadow's exploits became topical: when the New York Police were baffled by a real-life terrorist who signed himself "Three X," the Shadow met and conquered his fictional counterpart in the form of "Double Z" .... Most important, however, were the supervillains who developed during the Shadow's saga .... Always, when the Shadow defeated some monstrous scheme, he would be spurred on to tackle something bigger; while conversely, master criminals, learning that one of their ilk has been eliminated, would logically profit by that loss and devise something more powerful to thwart the Shadow.[37]

Naturally this vigilante-villain dialectic suggested a great deal more than economic or political "romance." Moral issues were involved. The plot structure of the typical avenger detective pulp defines the Christian dilemma of good versus evil. Forces easily identified as good, in a Christian sense, are pitted against demonic forces of evil in an apocalyptic struggle in which the very "Soul" of humanity is at stake. The avenger detective's adventures are an epic *Pilgrim's Progress* in which the road to salvation is led and guarded by the vigilante. The alternative to this road is damnation.

Metaphorically, the avenger detective's quest to the "super-villain's" underworld lair, which occurs with such formulaic regularity in the vigilante pulps that it becomes another motif complex, is akin to a descent into hell. In the Shadow's adventures, a favorite den of villainy is New York's Chinatown. The following excerpt from *The Teeth of the* in Dante's *Inferno*:

> The underworld headquarters of the Jeho Fan was the most grotesque meeting place that the Shadow had ever seen. Secreted among forgotten catacombs of Chinatown, its location was untraceable. Confident that the stronghold would ever be secure, the Jero Fan had spent a fortune in its embellishment. The result was a garish, hideous medley that resembled an opium smoker's nightmare.
>
> The square room illuminated by a sickly, greenlight glow. In that olive-tinged light, the Shadow saw monstrous faces peering down from every corner. They were huge statues, each of a Chinese joss, that stood as ten-foot guardians over the meetings of the Jero Fan.
>
> ...From that floor, more statues were visible, set between the giant images that stood in the corners. Some were figures of Chinese devils, slightly larger than lifesize. Others were dwarfish idols, squatted upon taborets.[38]

The inhabitants of such a place would call Satan friend:

> Two of the demons stepped from the side walls. They clamped hands upon the Shadow's shoulders, hauled him to his feet. Their hands were covered with heavy gauntlets, spiked with metal that dug through the prisoner's cloak. With a forward sweep, the pair sprawled the Shadow at the feet of the Tao Fan.
>
> The leader delivered an ugly, basso laugh. It brought a response from the devil-members. Their harsh mirth was loudened with the doomed room, giving it a demonic fury.[39]

The Shadow's escape from hell necessitates a heroic re-birth, a type of mythic regeneration through violence.

> The Shadow ran his doubled hand to his forehead. His forefinger dipped into the blood that still oozed slowly from the gash. The forefinger joined the others. The whole move of the Shadow's hand looked as he intended it. He had apparently reached to press a painful wound.
>
> Captors swung the Shadow to his feet. They were dragging him away, while the Tao and Ming Dwan watched as scorners. Then, from a pitiful, sagging slight, the Shadow became a power. His whole body whipped to action.
>
> His right forearm sliced upward; cracked the chin of the big false head and sent it flying, to reveal a wizened, baldish Chinaman instead. Twisting from the grip of those on the left, he drove in a hard punch toward the other captor on the right.[40]

The Depression, as a moral Depression (and not a political nor economic one), was a "real life" enactment of the apocalypse. The devil stood laughing in every bread line, and the country, as a whole, fell one notch deeper in the fiery pit each time a bank closed. America craved a

Christ-figure to combat this insidious moral decline. The pulp magazine publishers, sensing a market, produced dozens of avenger detective titles, totaling millions of copies sold, featuring the bloodthirsty vigilante who could battle his way out of hell in every issue. It was an allegory of its day which later proved to be the allegory of any day in which there was a perceived moral crisis.

The December, 1934 issue of *Operator 5* perhaps best illustrates the allegory of the apocalypse during America's "dark decade." Even the cover is fraught with conflict as titanic forces wage their war. A nattily-dressed Operator 5 places himself between an angry mob of blue-collar farm workers and a small group of cowering men and women. There is an older, distinguished looking man in the small group who could very well be any American banker or businessman. A young boy, no doubt Operator 5's dedicated assistant, Tim Donovan, stands at attention, ready to sacrifice his life if needed. Two attractive women, a blonde and a brunette, cringe behind Operator 5, representing in their own way the "flower" of WASP American womanhood. The threatened group stands on what appears to be the steps of a Washington monument, while in the distance, well behind the angry mob of farmers, a swirl of dust rises from a desolated farm, forming a black funnel-cloud in which there ride the Four Horsemen of the Apocalypse.

The story details the attempts of a madman named Apocryphos to achieve political domination of the United States. He develops a super-strain of deadly insects which devour the food reserves of the nation. He also employs a dark legion of fanatic followers who destroy warehouses and shipments of food. His ultimate goal is the starvation of the American people, which, of course, leads to political and social anarchy. Only the courage, strength and intelligence of America's Secret Service ace, Operator 5, halt the plans of Apocryphos, and as the magazine's blurb forecasts: "...only one man—Operator 5—realized the ghastly extent of the diabolical plot and only he... could hope to bring the canny schemer to the justice he deserved—death."[41]

Those monthly fictional apocalypses—pounded into that pulp paper, covered with garish chrome-stock illustrations, and selling for that thin dime—always ended happily ever after. Though cities fell and governments topped on the brink of disaster, the avenger detective hero never failed to save the day. This allegory suggested that with the proper heroic dimensions, the real-life apocalypse of the Depression, too, could be licked, the function of the sub-formula's second motif complex. Satan was overcome in every issue in the vigilante pulps, and there was never any "actual" fear for the readers of those stories that the "King of Darkness" would have the last laugh.

Notes

[1]T.Z. Lavine, *From Socrates to Sartre: The Philosophic Quest* (New York: Bantam, 1984), p. x.

[2]Edgar Allan Poe, "The Fall of the House of Usher," *The Annotated Tales of Edgar Allan Poe*, Stephen Peithman, ed., (Garden City: Doubleday, 1982), p. 77.

[3]Edgar Allan Poe, "The Murders in the Roe Morgue," *The Annotated Tales of Edgar Allan Poe*, Stephen Peithman, ed., (Garden City: Doubleday, 1982), p. 200.

[4]*Ibid.*

[5]*Ibid.*, pp. 200-201.

[6]*Ibid.*, p. 223.

[7]Peter L. Berger, *The Sacred Canopy: Elements of a Sociological Theory of Religion* (Garden City: Doubleday, 1967), p. 65.

[8]Chris Steinbrunner and Otto Penzler, *Encyclopedia of Mystery and Detection* (New York: McGraw-Hill, 1976), p. 403.

[9]George N. Dove, *The Police Procedural* (Bowling Green: Bowling Green University Popular Press, 1982), p. 2.

[10]Vidocq, "Victims of My Craft," *The World of Mystery Fiction*, Elliot L. Gilbert, ed., (Bowling Green: Bowling Green University Popular Press, 1983), p. 3.

[11]*Ibid.*, p. 4.

[12]Peter L. Berger and Thomas Luckmann, *The Social Construction of Reality* (Garden City: Doubleday, 1966), p. 77.

[13]*Ibid.*, p. 77.

[14]Vidocq, p. 12.

[15]Dove, p. 10.

[16]David K. Jeffrey, "Joseph Wambaugh," *Twentieth-Century Crime and Mystery Writers*, John M. Reilly, ed., (New York: St. Martin's Press, 1980), p.441.

[17]Berger, p. 86.

[18]William F. Nolan, *The Black Mask Boys* (New York: Morrow, 1985), p. 19.

[19]*Ibid.*, p. 20.

[20]*Ibid.*, p. 22.

[21]*Ibid.*, p. 36.

[22]*Ibid.*

[23]*Ibid.*

[24]*Ibid.*, p. 35.

[25]Carroll John Daly, "Three Gun Terry," *The Black Mask Boys*, William F. Nolan, ed., (New York: Morrow, 1985), p. 43.

[26]*Ibid.*, pp. 43-44.

[27]*Ibid.*, p. 44.

[28]Berger and Luckmann, p. 171.

[29]Daly, p. 44.

[30]Berger, p. 33.

[31]Robert B. Parker, "Dashiell Hammett," *Twentieth-Century Crime and Mystery Writers*, John M. Reilly, ed., (New York: St. Martin's Press, 1980), p. 286.

[32]*Ibid.*, p. 286.

[33]Robert Sampson, *The Night Master* (Chicago: The Pulp Press, 1982), pp. 25-30.

[34]Maxwell Grant (Walter Gibson), *The Crime Oracle and The Teeth of the Dragon* (New York: Dover, 1975), p. ix.

[35]Robert Weinberg and Lohr McKinstry, *The Hero Pulp Index* (Evergreen: Opar Press, 1971), pp. 1-48.

[36]Berger, p. 91.

[37]Maxwell Grant (Walter Gibson), "The Shadow," *The Great Pulp Detectives*, Otto Penzler, ed., (London: Penguin, 1978), pp. 210-215.

[38]Maxwell Grant (Walter Gibson), *The Crime Oracle and The Teeth of the Dragon* (New York: Dover, 1975), pp. 210-215.

[39]*Ibid.*, p. 122.

[40]*Ibid.*, p. 125.

[41]*Operator 5*, "The Legions of Starvation," (Dec., 1934), Vol. 3, No. 1.

CONCLUSION

THIS STUDY HAS CONSTRUCTED a bridge between the social sciences on the one hand and the humanities on the other. The value of this type of methodological approach combines the best qualities of both disciplines. Recognizing various myth/symbol structures in literature is a valuable way to identify those elements of a story that reflect certain important aspects of a culture. But culture is a product of society and social processes. By not establishing a connection to sociology, specifically the sociology of knowledge, the myth/symbol approach becomes more of a literary exercise and less of a study of society. Sociology provides the basic "tools" for the study of mythmaking in fiction, but rarely do scholars of the discipline use these tools in the humanities, such as applying reality construction to the writing and reading of popular stories. Humanities oriented scholars may recognize alienation in the hard-boiled sub-formula of the mystery genre, for example, but by not defining alienation as a social factor, they confuse the meaning of the term. Sociologists may define alienation and apply that definition to work environments and family structures, but by not looking at its use in popular fiction, which, after all, is simply another product of society, they miss an opportunity to uncover a mass social expression as it is revealed in the print entertainment medium. Humanities scholars who study the formulas and sub-formulas of the mystery genre may recognize the life and death struggle between the protagonist of the story and his environment; sociologists who study the death crisis and its effect on individual conduct in social organizations may advance the importance of the death crisis in those organizations: this study has presented an argument that unites the two disciplines, suggesting that the mystery genre features six formulas that align across a spectrum between rational explanations of life and death and irrational explanations. In these six formulas, the protagonist's control (or lack of control) of the death crisis illustrates significant social concerns and social constructions of reality. With the six formulas, a historical taxonomy has been outlined of various sub-formulas, using the descriptive techniques of literary criticism to highlight the social-psychological function of mystery formula construction, which subsequently details the dynamic interaction of the individual with social environment, institutions and culture. This method of looking at popular fiction (and the definitions of the formulas and sub-formulas of the mystery genre as an important segment of popular culture) suggests a new language of social/literary analysis, a language that acknowledges the socially defining, democratizing experience of the print entertainment mass medium.

BIBLIOGRAPHY

Aisenberg, Nadya. *A Common Spring: Crime Novel & Classic.* Bowling Green: Bowling Green University Popular Press, 1979.

Ashley, Mike. *Who's Who in Horror and Fantasy Fiction.* New York: Taplinger Publishing Co., 1977.

Ball, John, ed. *The Mystery Story.* Del Mar: University of California, San Diego, 1976.

Benson, Raymond. *The James Bond Bedside Companion.* New York: Dodd, Mead, 1984.

Berger, Peter L. *The Sacred Canopy: Elements of a Sociological Theory of Religion.* Garden City: Doubleday, 1967.

Berger, Peter L. and Luckmann, Thomas. *The Social Construction of Reality.* Garden City: Doubleday, 1966.

Bloch, Robert. *Psycho.* New York: Bantam, 1959.

Boorstin, Daniel J. *The Americans: The Democratic Experience.* New York: Random House, 1973.

Bowden, Jan A., ed. *Contemporary Authors: Volumes 65-68.* Detroit: Gale Research, 1977.

Cain, James M. *The Postman Always Rings Twice.* New York: Grosset & Dunlap, 1934.

Cawelti, John G. *Adventure, Mystery, and Romance.* Chicago: University of Chicago Press, 1976.

Davis, Peter. *The American Heritage Dictionary of the English Language.* New York: Dell, 1976.

Dove, George N. *The Police Procedural.* Bowling Green: Bowling Green University Popular Press, 1982.

Fleming, Ian. *Casino Royale.* New York: Signet, 1953.

Gilbert, Elliot L. *The World of Mystery Fiction.* Bowling Green: Bowling Green University Popular Press, 1983.

Grant, Maxwell. *The Crime Oracle and the Teeth of the Dragon.* New York: Dover, 1975.

Haining, Peter. *Terror: A History of Horror Illustrations From the Pulp Magazines.* New York: A & W Visual Library, 1976.

Haining, Peter, ed. *Vampires at Midnight.* New York: Grosset &

Dunlap, 1970.

Hanshew, Thomas W. *Cleek: The Man of Forty Faces.* New York: McKinlay, Stone & Mackenzie, 1918.

Haycraft, Howard. *Murder for Pleasure: The Life and Times of the Detective Story.* New York: Carroll & Graf Publishers, 1984.

Herman, Linda and Stiel, Beth. *Corpus Delicti of Mystery Fiction: A Guide to the Body of the Case.* Metuchen: Scarecrow, 1974.

Hornung, E.W. *The Amateur Cracksman.* New York: Scribner's, 1910.

Johannsen, Albert. *The House of Beadle and Adams, and its Dime and Nickle Novels.* Norman: University of Oklahoma Press, 1950.

Kallich, Martin. *Horace Walpole.* New York: Twayne Publishers, 1971.

Keating, H.R.F. *Whodunit? A Guide to Crime, Suspense and Spy Fiction.* New York: Van Nostrand Reinhold, 1982.

Kittredge, William and Krauzer, Steven M., eds. *The Great American Detective.* New York: Mentor, 1978.

Lavine, T.Z. *From Socrates to Sartre: The Philosophic Quest.* New York: Bantam, 1984.

LeCarre, John. *The Incongruous Spy.* New York: Walker & Co., 1961.

Levi-Strauss, Claude. *Structural Anthopology.* New York: Basic Books, 1963.

Lewis, R.W.B. *The American Adam: Innocence, Tragedy and Tradition in the Nineteenth Century.* Chicago: University of Chicago Press, 1955.

Lovecraft, H.P. *Dagon and Other Macabre Tales.* Sauk City: Arkham House, 1965.

McBain, Howard Lee. *Prohibition Legal and Illegal.* New York: Macmillan, 1928.

Nolan, William F. *The Black Mask Boys.* New York: Morrow, 1985.

Panek, LeRoy L. *The Special Branch: The British Spy Novel, 1890-1980.* Bowling Green: Bowling Green University Popular Press, 1981.

Penzler, Otto, ed. *The Great Detectives.* London: Penguin, 1978.

Poe, Edgar Allan. *The Annotated Tales of Edgar Allan Poe.* Garden City: Doubleday, 1982.

Puzo, Mario. *The Godfather.* New York: Putnam's, 1969.

Reilly, John M., ed. *Twentieth-Century Crime and Mystery Writers.* New York: St. Martin's Press, 1980.

Roberts, Garyn G. "The Many Faces of Dick Tracy." Master's Thesis, Bowling Green State University, 1983.

Sampson, Robert. *Yesterday's Faces: Glory Figures.* Bowling Green: Bowling Green University Popular Press, 1983.

Sampson, Robert. *The Night Master.* Chicago: The Pulp Press, 1982.

Slotkin, Richard. *Regeneration Through Violence: The Mythology of the American Frontier, 1600-1860.* Middletown: Wesleyan University Press, 1973.

Smith, Henry Nash. *Virgin Land: The American West as Symbol and Myth.* Cambridge: Harvard University Press, 1950.

Tracy, Ann B. *The Gothic Novel: 1790-1830.* Lexington: University of Kentucky Press, 1981.

Turner, Frederick Jackson. *The Significance of the Frontier in American History.* New York: Frederick Ungar, 1963.

Van Cise, Philip S. *Fighting the Underworld.* Boston: Houghton Mifflin, 1936.

Varma, Devendra P. *The Gothic Flame.* London: Arthur Barker, 1957.

Walpole, Horace. *The Castle of Otranto: A Gothic Story.* London: Oxford University Press, 1964.

Weinberg, Robert and McKinstry, Lohr. *The Hero Pulp Index.* Evergreen: Opar Press, 1971.

Woolrich, Cornell. *The Bride Wore Black.* New York: Ballantine, 1984.